RETURN TO A CHINESE VILLAGE

Titles in Pantheon's series of reports from villages throughout the world are

After Hitler: Report from a West German City, by Jürgen Neven–du Mont (1969)

Akenfield: Portrait of an English Village, by Ronald Blythe (1969)

Amoskeag: Life and Work in an American Factory-City, by Tamara Hareven and Randolph Langenbach (1978)

Change at Shebika: Report from a North African Village, by Jean Duvignaud (1970)

China: The Revolution Continued, by Jan Myrdal and Gun Kessle (1970)

Division Street: America, by Studs Terkel (1966)

In the Fist of the Revolution: Life in a Cuban Country Town, by Jose Yglesias (1968)

Kibbutz Makom, by Amia Leiblich (1981)

Longtime Californ': A Documentary Study of an American Chinatown, by Victor G. Nee and Brett de Bary Nee (1973)

Maps and Dreams, by Hugh Brody (1982)

Off the Middle Way: Report from a Swedish Village, by Sture Källberg (1973)

The Red and the White: Report from a French Village, by Edgar Morin (1970)

Report from a Chinese Village, by Jan Myrdal (1965)

Shinohata: A Portrait of a Japanese Village, by Ronald P. Dore (1978)

Sicilian Lives, by Danilo Dolci (1982)

Tajos: The Story of a Village on the Costa del Sol, by Ronald Fraser (1973)

Ten Mile Inn: Mass Movement in a Chinese Village, by Isabel and David Crook (1979)

RETURN TO A CHINESE VILLAGE

JAN MYRDAL

Photographs by Gun Kessle

Foreword by Harrison E. Salisbury

Translated from the Swedish by Alan Bernstein

PANTHEON BOOKS
New York

Library of Congress Cataloging in Publication Data
Myrdal, Jan.
    Return to a Chinese village.
    Translation of: Kinesisk by 20 år senare.
    1. Liu-lin (China)—Social conditions. 2. China—Politics and government—1976– . 3. China—Rural conditions. 4. Villages—China—Case studies.
I. Title.
HN740.L58M9613   1984   306'.0951   83-24976
ISBN 0-394-53774-2
ISBN 0-394-72453-4 (pbk.)

Manufactured in the United States of America
First American Edition

It has been many years since the peasants have been as happy as they are today.

—Hu Yaobang, September 1, 1982,
Chinese Communist Party Central Committee
report to the Twelfth Party Congress

CONTENTS

Contents

ILLUSTRATIONS

Illustrations

(Between pages 98 and 99)

Liu Lin village, 1982.

The fields that were terraced and prepared for tractor cultivation during the Cultural Revolution are now being divided up between the groups and transformed into small private plots.

The new main street in Liu Lin village. The People's Commune administration complex is on the right.

Party Secretary Li Qisheng.

Households are beginning to buy small hand tractors for hauling.

The workshop now manufactures iron beds from the material that was to be used to make sprinkler systems. The market decides.

From Liu Lin the peasants take their products to be sold at the free market in Yanan.

Wang Yulan, *minban* teacher (paid by the brigade) since 1978.

Li Hongfu's grandchild during a Chinese lesson in the second grade.

The masses, the health-care workers, and the party in Liu Lin have decided not to discard the collective medical-care system. The health insurance system is maintained.

Luo Hanhong.

Cao Zhengui.

FOREWORD

When Jan Myrdal told Mao Zedong on October 1, 1962, that he had just spent a month studying the northern Shaanxi village of Liu Lin, Mao was appalled: "They never should have sent you there. It's too backward." But, Myrdal objected, Liu Lin possessed "a revolutionary tradition." Mao guffawed and waved Myrdal on down the receiving line at the Great Hall of the People.

Mao seemed to be right. Liu Lin (Willow Grove) nestled in the deeply eroded Shaanxi loess country, a stone's throw from the Red Revolutionary capital of Yanan, was hardly the place for serious study of Chinese peasant life, Communist organization of agriculture, or the role of the party in changing the face of China.

And, yet, time and Myrdal's stubborn dedication to his task were to demonstrate that Mao's dismissal of the idea of "learning from Liu Lin" was far too hasty. In the two decades since Myrdal's first visit to that remote, dusty corner of China we have learned a great deal from Liu Lin—of the peasants, of Communist agricultural policy, of China, and, not least, of Jan Myrdal himself. They have all changed. It is the angles of the intersection of these changes that provide us with the most valuable insights.

It is in the angles of change (and coincidence) that are exposed in Myrdal's successive visits to Liu Lin that his contribution is most illuminating. Two things were in constant process of evolution: Liu Lin and its response to the successive policies and programs of the Chinese Communist Revolution, and Myrdal with his own intellectual transitions (and lack of transitions).

These factors award an extraordinary interest to Myrdal's continuing observation of this dusty north Shaanxi village and provide some fixed points upon which we can base our study of the whole China experiment.

Myrdal's *Report from a Chinese Village*, published in the United States in 1965 (in Sweden *Rapport från kinesisk,* 1963), was and remains a classic. Myrdal brought to it precisely those ingredients that gave his findings depth and illumination. He was, as he was careful to explain, a radical intellectual, strongly biased by his Swedish heritage and by the particularity of descent on his father's side from the village of Solvarbo in Dalecarlia, a region of the stoutest peasant tradition. He has since childhood strongly identified with the peasant cause. He was at pains to warn his readers of this Dalecarlian influence and his tendency to view the Chinese peasants through Solvarbo lenses.

He had made his approach to China from the Asian side—serious socioeconomic-political studies in India, Afghanistan, and Burma. He brought no expertise in Chinese questions to his study of Liu Lin, but he came with a pack stuffed with background books and his mind swirling with images of Asian peasants and Dalecarlian laborers. He was, as he strongly suggested in his introduction to *Report,* eager and ready to discover that China had "solved" her peasant problem.

It was no doubt Myrdal's awareness of his own bias as well as the painstaking detail that he extracted from the interviews he and his talented wife, Gun, conducted in their month's stay in Liu Lin that gave *Report* its solidity, its fine fabric, its photographic and phonographic realism. *Report* is an impressive piece of work. No serious account of the Chinese countryside in the interval between the Great Leap Forward and the Great Proletarian Cultural Revolution can be written without confronting Myrdal's work. Much of its strength derives from simplicity of structure. He bases himself on clear, detailed interviews, and he presents statistics and background in succinct, almost laconic fashion. There is a notable absence of rhetoric, but Myrdal never lets you doubt that he believes the Chinese, the village, and the commune have found the right track. He himself is not shy of appearing in the narrative.

As Myrdal then said: "The usefulness of this book to the reader in his search for reality and the validity of my whole argument rests of course on my honesty . . . my bias is primarily that of an intellectual and humanitarian tradition. My premise is that human beings are in the last analysis rational, that they respond in a rational manner to an existing social and material reality.

"The pride of this tradition is that you change your opinion as the facts outgrow them, as the snake changes its skin. You are constant not in your opinion but in your receptivity to factual information."

Jan Myrdal visited Liu Lin in 1962, 1969, 1974, 1978, and 1982. The product of these trips has been three books—the initial *Report*; a second study, *China: The Revolution Continued* (in Swedish, *Kina: Revolutionen går vidare*) in 1970; and the present volume. In addition, he wrote a television script on his 1978 visit.

For a village of about 1,000 population Liu Lin has become extremely well documented. The first foreigner to visit and write about it was the late Edgar Snow in 1960. It was Myrdal's reading of Snow's account of Liu Lin (Willow Grove) that brought him there in 1962. Others have reported on Willow Grove. I visited it in 1972. A group of Swedish tourists saw it in 1980, and Haldore Hanson, a veteran AP correspondent, saw it in 1983. (To be technical, Liu Lin is actually a work brigade that encompasses four small villages.)

Typical or not, Liu Lin has become by chance a kind of barometer of Chinese agriculture, Chinese village life, and Chinese attitudes. Mao may have had reason to guffaw in 1962, but Myrdal, quite clearly, will have the last laugh.

The existence of what amounts to a control body of evidence adds piquancy to Myrdal's reports because these reports can be construed not only as progress charts on Liu Lin but as landmarks in the evolution of the philosophy of Myrdal himself.

If a flaw was to be found in *Report,* it lay not in the meticulous examination of village life, in the portraits of the villagers, the improvement of their living conditions, their sense of achievement, or their optimism about the future. The flaw lay in the manner in which Liu Lin was presented, almost *in vitro,* largely isolated from such events as the Let One Hundred Flowers Bloom movement and even the Great Leap Forward. The Leap was described in benign terms, with no hint, as we now know, and as the realistic and skeptical Shaanxi peasants must have known from the beginning, of its disastrous results, the ridiculous construction of "backyard steel furnaces" and the like.

If this was a venial sin in Myrdal's 1962 report, it laid a foundation for something more serious when he returned to Liu Lin in 1969. In those seven years China had been swept by the Great Proletarian Cultural Revolution. The state had come within an ace of foundering in the anarchic storms. Its leadership had been torn apart, millions had lost their lives, the industrial structure had been brought to a halt, education shut its doors for ten years. The violence had far from ceased.

To come to China in 1969 was like venturing onto a battlefield during a lull in the fighting, the air still laden with gunpowder, fires burning dully, bodies not yet buried, an ominous threat that at any moment combat will again break out.

Perhaps this is what gave Myrdal's 1969 book its angry quality. He had taken his side for what he thought were the principles of the Cultural Revolution. He urged his readers to turn to Mao's *Little Red Book* for answers and to read Lin Biao's famous text on guerilla warfare. In reporting on Liu Lin, Myrdal told faithfully of the new procedures brought in by the Cultural Revolution, changes in leadership (the "Old Secretary," Li Youhua, hero of *Report,* had died of cancer). But he also spent much time arguing with critics or supposed critics. (The United States, the Soviet Union, "misinformation about China," in general, and a dozen reports in particular.) He announced angrily: "The reader might say that I am biased in favor of China and the cultural revolution. Of course I am. Nobody can read what I have written these last years without seeing this; the rational, and in my opinion, necessary determining reasons are contained in what I have written. And of course I have changed."

Despite this noisy polemic, Myrdal continued to do his job. He talked to the people of Liu Lin and he reported what they told him and, so far as one can see, he set out these views plain and unvarnished. What he did not do, however, was to attempt the broader assessment he had made seven years before.

He reported—flatly and without emphasis—the single most significant fact about Liu Lin—that it did not enter the Cultural Revolution until September 15, 1968, two years and five weeks after it had been proclaimed. (Myrdal used the date of August 8,

1966, but, of course, the Revolution had actually been underway since early 1966.)

What this meant was that Liu Lin, far from possessing, as Myrdal had thought in 1962, a "noble revolutionary heritage," was actually a stubborn, reserved, show-me community very typical of the Chinese countryside. It was happy to move forward, but it moved with "all deliberate caution." It did not put duncecaps on its party leaders and stone them in the streets. It did not drive out "Capitalist Roaders" and other imagined enemies. It indulged in the mildest kind of self-criticism and then went ahead, plowing its fields, cultivating its new orchards, improving its irrigation system, trying to get its machine shop to work better. In a word it practiced Production, not Revolution, and this was anethema to the goals of the Cultural Revolution. If Myrdal thought in 1969 that Liu Lin was a product of the Cultural Revolution, he was badly mistaken. And if, as is quite clear, he believed in the words, slogans, and decrees of the Cultural Revolution (it is by no means clear how much he really knew of what was going on in China in those years), then that dedication he repeatedly proclaimed to the proposition that human beings are "in the last analysis rational" was sadly distorted by the violent, contagious mania, paranoia, and dementia that had begun to flow through China.

The extraordinary point that Myrdal's interviews in Liu Lin in 1969 demonstrate is the rationality of the peasantry and its ability to carry on, virtually unaffected by the howling winds of the Cultural Revolution that Myrdal so vigorously embraced (again, it must be submitted, he probably was not aware of the dark events of the period).

If the flaw in Myrdal's *Report* had been minor (his failure to relate Liu Lin seriously to such movements as the Hundred Flowers and the Great Leap), the flaw in his 1969 book was critical because here he accepted the rhetoric, the slogans of the Cultural Revolution and attributed the evolving agricultural economy and social well-being of Liu Lin to the *Little Red Book*. He saw this as the final triumph of the Revolution in the countryside. In reality, as time would show, the Cultural Revolution had demonstrated the virtual immunity of the countryside to any sloganeering that did not promise better harvests, more material benefits, higher wages, more household goods, and so on.

The tone and quality of Myrdal's 1978 script for the Liu Lin TV documentary is relaxed, almost congratulatory. Gone are the polemics of the Cultural Revolution. Gone are the pistol shots at enemies lurking on the horizon—the Russians, the Americans, critics in Sweden. He was forty-two in 1969. By 1978 he was fifty-one, more mellow, relaxed, a middle-aged political scientist, not an angry young man. There are no polemics in 1978, just even-handed prose. Liu Lin is prospering. It has cut its wheat production back and increased the area for forestry. Its machine shop is turning out spare parts and developing nicely. The noodle factory is going great guns. Its by-products feed the pigs. Incomes are rising. There are no real problems. Liu Lin is still a distant village in the Shaanxi loess, but it is leagues ahead of those primitive caves of the early 1930s. The political leader of Liu Lin, Feng Changye (he was the man who escorted me around in 1972; he had been a leader in 1962; he still is today), was firmly in charge. No real political changes had occurred, not during the Cultural Revolution, not during the regime of the Gang of Four, not in the aftermath of Mao Zedong's death, not in the rise of Deng Xiaoping. Myrdal was beginning to recognize the political and social stability of Liu Lin. Myrdal did not seem to find anything incompatible between the Liu Lin of 1978 and that which he had envisaged evolving under the aegis of the Cultural Revolution in 1969. Was this an accurate observation? Or was a new phenomenon beginning to take place? Were, in fact, Myrdal and Liu Lin beginning to age together?

Now in 1982 Jan Myrdal, accompanied as always by his wife, Gun, and her camera, has returned to Liu Lin and what he finds there as he tells us has aroused his "misgivings." The picture he presents, he believes, is a correct one: "I would like to believe that it isn't. But I believe that it is."

What has happened? Well, one can search Myrdal's actual statistics on Liu Lin, his talks with the leaders of Liu Lin (long since they have become if not old friends, at least old, old acquaintances). He gives us what they say. Production moves forward. There are no changes of consequence in leadership. Feng Changye is still in charge. The men and women running Liu Lin are all old hands. We have met them before. Some things are on the decline—the machine shop, for example. It looks as though it might go out of business. Whether policy or bad management is responsible is hard to tell. Some plans have been abandoned. Yanan is pushing out and Liu Lin is growing into a suburb. Local facilities are declining. It is easier to shop in Yanan. There is a plan for a railroad, which will rob Liu Lin of some good agricultural fields. It does not look as though Liu Lin's agricultural future will be brighter, partly because of urbanization, partly, perhaps, because of the new profit-oriented agricultural policies. But here Myrdal reports a significant fact. It was not until 1981 that Liu Lin finally went over to the new "family responsibility" plan. It stayed with the old brigade and workteam for nearly five years after the rest of the country started to change over. Once again, Myrdal demonstrates Liu Lin's basic conservatism, but he doesn't seem to recognize that this provides the central theme of the Liu Lin saga. Liu Lin wasn't very revolutionary at the start. It never has been. It changes slowly and reluctantly.

But this is not what interests Myrdal. He is looking far beyond Liu Lin. What interests him is Mao Zedong and the Great Cultural Revolution. He still believes in both; that is, he believes in the radical revolutionary policies of the Cultural Revolution and in the Mao of the *Little Red Book*. It is almost as though all of China had moved forward under Deng Xiaoping while Myrdal lingers in the past (the vanguard, he would feel), calling on China to return to those rhetorical slogans, those hyperradical policies that brought it so close to chaos.

He has not, he insists, changed. "My basic outlook," he says, "is the same as that of the fifteen-year-old who forty years ago read *Red Star over China*." If this be so, the most romantic of revolutionary images must persist in the fifty-five-year-old Myrdal. He defends what he calls Mao's policy of sending intellectuals down to the countryside to mind the pigs. He does not touch on the suicides, the murders, the killings, the torture. He defends the sending of millions of young Red Guards to the countryside but utters no word for the damage to the country's scientific and technological elite. He envisages Mao's slogans as inspiring revolutionary causes thousands of years hence.

Myrdal is now at ripe middle age. His central philosophy may well still be rooted in an adolescent response to Snow's *Red Star*. He must be one of the very last individuals to preserve positive images of the Cultural Revolution in (apparently) all of its convolutions, although I still doubt Myrdal has ever informed himself of what *really* happened during that era.

What can one say? With it all, his reports and observations achieve remarkable power. Almost against his will he shows us the eternal continuity of Liu Lin, its ability to survive *any* political turn or twist and move forward. If fate decrees that it shall become a suburb of Yanan, so be it—the people will continue their work, rigorously and with profit to themselves (Haldore Hanson saw Liu Lin in 1983 and did not feel it was becoming suburbanized). The peasants move like the Yellow River, which flows through that same loess land—irresistibly, relentlessly.

And Myrdal: We are in his debt for painstaking reporting and more. He makes vivid criticisms of the post-Mao China, criticisms that can only come from a true believer in what he assumes to have been Mao's political theses. Myrdal has called his 1982 visit his "last" report on Liu Lin. He does not believe that he will return again. The political gap between himself and the regime of Deng Xiaoping is too great. But that may not hold true. China changes, but more slowly than Myrdal would have it. But it does change. He has changed a great deal, too, and in that change has given us insights both new and old of great social and political value. And a candid look at a passionate political pilgrim, himself, still wrestling with the eternal problems of truth, of goals, of the nature of mankind.

Harrison E. Salisbury

PREFACE

In 1982 I visited China for the sixth time. I first came to China in 1962 from an India plagued by rural famine. In this interval I have spent a total of twenty-three months in China—traveling or writing. When writing I have lived in Peking or Qingdao. *Lived* is perhaps the wrong word; I was in Peking and I was in Qingdao.

Since the war years when I first read Edgar Snow's *Red Star over China,* I have made efforts to understand developments in China. For me as for many others, Mao Zedong and Yanan provided the inspiration, hope, and conviction of the feasibility of Communism, long before liberation in 1949. Yanan held a greater symbolic value for me than did Stalingrad toward the end of the Second World War. Books such as Hogg's *I See a New China* had a great influence on me. Later, during the war against the KMT (Guomindang), I sat in Stockholm translating into Swedish the Xinhua reports coming (I believe) via Jack Chen in London.

While engaged in international antiimperialist youth work after the war, I came to know Chinese comrades. The most gifted of them, Zhen Dawei (one of the Chinese Youth Association's most promising cadres), is reported to be dead. (It is said that he died of a heart attack in the countryside. A natural death. Not from maltreatment or persecution.)

In this way China has meant a lot to me. But this does not mean that I claim to know a great deal about it, even if I have tried to describe Chinese reality and Chinese developments as accurately as possible. Ever since I first began to form political opinions in my middle teens, I have regarded the Chinese people's great revolution as the decisive event of this century. I have never had cause to revise this belief. Yet I have never seen myself as a "China expert" or a "specialist." China is exceedingly large. My knowledge is limited. My field of vision encompasses only a small portion of the everyday life of the 1 billion Chinese.

In 1982 I traveled once more in China. I visited again—the

fifth time—Liu Lin brigade. As I describe this and other visits, report discussions and issues, and attempt to summarize my view on the developments of these decades, my basic outlook is the same as that of the fifteen-year-old who forty years ago read *Red Star over China*. The world is not a chessboard where great powers play against each other; in the end it is the people who determine history. I am convinced I am right about this. I might be wrong about other things, make incorrect observations, come to mistaken conclusions.

The analysis presented in this final report takes Liu Lin Brigade as an example (I am able to speak of Liu Lin with some assurance), but it also attempts to shed light upon developments in Liu Lin by means of information, discussions, and material from other places. I believe that the picture that ultimately emerges is correct. I would like to hope that it isn't. But I believe it is.

Jan Myrdal
Nice, France, 1982

RETURN TO A CHINESE VILLAGE

PREMISES

The November 4, 1982 edition of the French journal *TEL* reports that Pekingologists at the Academy of Sciences in Moscow have compiled an internal reference study on Lin Biao, according to which he and his wife, Ye Qun, were executed in the seaside resort of Beidaihe and were not aboard the airplane that crashed in Mongolia on September 13, 1971. It is possible that this is Soviet disinformation, or that such a document from the Academy of Science does not exist, or that such a document does, in fact, exist and that it is correctly reported, and, what is more, that the information is correct. These are interesting possibilities to discuss. But they are of only marginal significance for anyone interested in understanding China's development.

Just how important personal struggles and intrigues among the Chinese leadership are depends on to what extent the various protagonists reflect genuine social forces. Leaders do not lead. If Lin Biao (or the Gang of Four, for that matter) for a short time appeared to lead the masses, they found themselves in a situation similar to that of Chaplin's in *Modern Times* when he picks up the red warning flag and suddenly finds himself the leader of a demonstration.

The only genuine leader of the masses to emerge in China during the last decades—and one who is still able to lead long after his own death—is Mao Zedong. And he led by not leading. Even in the midst of the great homage that declared him leader, he was able to see the absurdity of leadership. It is said that when Zhou Enlai told him of Lin Biao's flight to the Soviet Union, Mao Zedong answered: "One cannot stop the rain from falling; one cannot stop a woman from marrying another. Let him do what he wants!"

Provided that he actually did say just that just then, and that Lin Biao really did try to escape.

To be sure, political decisions made on high are of importance. Decisions as to the purchase price of grain and directives concerning party work in conjunction with the dissolution of collectives do have their impact. But the decisions taken at the center do not govern developments; they act as reinforcement and feedback for strong forces already in existence. They reflect the class struggle and, in turn, serve to shape and further that struggle.

China's future will not be determined in Peking, even though the individual or group holding central power this year or that does matter for China's development.

America's leading Pekingologist, John King Fairbanks, the man who has trained two generations of China experts and who has had, and still has, a great influence over the way in which China and Chinese developments are presently described in the United States and countries within Washington's sphere, has spoken scornfully of those who report from the pigpens. He regards the Chinese intellectuals as the leading and important force in China. This view he shares with the Chinese bureaucratic intellectuals reared in a 2,000-year-old mandarin tradition. The intellect governs, the hand obeys. I, on the other hand, believe that it is the way to the pigsty, the view from the bottom up, that provides the grand, the human, perspective, and that it is the traditional intellectuals who are narrow-minded, ignorant, and struck with blindness, even if they have become Communists and responsible cadres. Mao Zedong wished them to free themselves to become latrine emptiers and pig keepers, tasks that did not demand the physical strength needed for normal farmwork and that, consequently, could be left in the villages to feeble old people and the intellectuals from the cities.

This is considered to be one of Mao Zedong's most heinous crimes against humanity by Chinese officials (and their confrères in both the United States and Soviet Union, as well as in all the countries within the sphere of influence of the superpowers). But it was what Gandhi, too, demanded. Brahmins and mandarins, both groups reared in ancient traditions of learning, could develop into true intellectuals only by breaking caste.

Mao Zedong's other great crime in the minds of traditional intellectuals was that he urged young people to break with parents and family and to go out into the countryside and take up the struggle themselves. He urged them to go west. He encouraged them to set out on long marches through the country, in order that they might know China's greatness and the greatness of the Chinese people, and not just sit like sticks-in-the-mud within the narrow confines of Peking or Shanghai. He incited them to destroy the influence of Confucianism and its false propriety.

And, what is more, he, as Communist Party leader, did what no Communist party leader in any country could forgive: he spurred the masses to criticism and he called into question the party itself. It was headquarters that was to be bombarded. And in the prolongation of that thought could be seen the insight that although the party was a necessary tool for the achievement of national liberation and social revolution, afterward it automatically began to transform itself into an apparatus of oppression and to excrete a new class in a new type of fascist state such as that found in the Soviet Union. In opposing such a transformation, it is right to revolt, even if this revolt is directed against party organization and party leadership. And it was in his role of party leader, having control over various central power organs (gained by way of various shifting power struggles), that Mao Zedong was able to urge the bombardment of headquarters and hinder the attempts of the party apparatus to strike back.

Mao Zedong has made a contribution of historic and worldwide significance by liberating and formulating the thousand-year-old demands of China's poor peasantry, while simultaneously liberating and formulating the hopes of the rebellious young students, and by uniting these demands with the great tradition of popular Chinese Taoism and the culminating formulation of European tradition (Marx's leap from utopian socialism to scientific socialism). Here runs a dividing line across our time: before Mao and after Mao. Politics can never go back to conditions existing before Mao, just as economics has never been able to return to the situation preceding Marx, or biology to the situation preceding Darwin. This is regardless of what one might think of these highly distinguished men.

In the great and ongoing revolutionary movement, where it will remain acceptable to make revolution for thousands and tens of thousands of years, Mao Zedong's work will endure. But throughout this entire epoch one line will continue to conceal another, right and left will change places: power will shift guise; party leaders, politicians, and generals will struggle for power, and the masses continue to impel the wheel of history forward. The Gang of Four tried to float along up on top. But they couldn't keep it up. They just weren't fit. All they could do was make slogans. Mao Zedong tried to make use of them. But his tools cracked. They were unable to play a genuine leftist role. Mao Zedong had high hopes for Wang Hongwen. He permitted him to gain power and opportunities. But Wang Hongwen proved himself incapable when he had to deal with real-life social struggles in Hangzhou. He fled from the difficult decisions. He thought himself powerful and left to go fishing. Back in Hangzhou he left chaos that did not develop into effective revolt. Mao Zedong was forced to call in the adroit bureaucrat and military leader Deng Xiaoping and send him to Hangzhou. He put down that which Wang Hongwen was unable to develop. Then Mao Zedong let Wang Hongwen go ahead. Wang was dazzled by the exalted position he had attained in the world's most populous nation and surrounded himself with luxury. But he had not withstood the test and his position was temporary. Mao Zedong understood what the future would bring. The left was unfit for the task. Its leaders were nowhere to be seen. The right had leaders. It would be the right that took over. But eventually everything would inexorably turn again. The time would come when the masses would revolt against the right. But that might be long after his own death, and new generations solve their problems their own way.

Mao Zedong was old and knew that he was dying. He was only able to work and read a few hours a day. His mind was clear at that time. The rest of the time he was tired. Just before the death of Zhou Enlai, Mao said to him: "Now that the country has become red, who is its guardian? The task that was ours remains unfinished, it might take another thousand years. The struggle has taxed our strength and our hair has turned gray. Old friend! Can you and I remain spectators while our efforts are swept away?"

Following the death of Zhou Enlai, Mao Zedong attempted one last time to come up with a constellation of personalities that would allow a standoff of the various political forces until the time when the left would have grown strong and developments could have taken a new leap. With Hua Guofeng in charge, Mao Zedong could feel assured that China's rural areas would continue to learn from Dazhai, the model that was established at great cost to the state to serve as showcase brigade and reception center for millions of Chinese peasants (and several thousand foreign visitors) who had come to learn since 1963. The eighty-three families in this poor brigade were to serve as an object lesson illustrating Mao Zedong's teaching on "the old man who removed the mountains." Hard, purposeful work could achieve anything. Mao Zedong's directive from 1964—"In agriculture learn from Dazhai!"—later became standard policy during the Cultural Revolution, and Dazhai's party secretary, Chen Yonggui, became a Politburo member, the only member with long experience of physical labor. Mao Zedong knew that Eua Guofeng was prepared to adhere to these basic principles.

The criticism of Dazhai by the Chinese press in 1980 was similar to that made by cadres close to Liu Shaoqi right from the start of the campaign: the model brigade Dazhai cost the state money. I found that standpoint about as relevant as a critical remark to the effect that agricultural colleges receive subsidies from the state.

Hua Guofeng's adherence to Mao Zedong's line and his insistence that what Mao Zedong had said and done was correct and remained the proper guide to action was later branded a deviation from true Mao Zedong Thought. This is now referred to as the struggle against "the two whatevers." This expression first appeared in an editorial in *The People's Daily* of February 7, 1977, approved by Hua Guofeng: "We shall resolutely stand up in defense of all the political decisions made by Chairman Mao; we shall unswervingly conform to all instructions given by Chairman Mao." In Chinese both sentences begin with the words *Fanshi Mao zhuxi . . . ,* or "Whatever Chairman Mao . . ."

Hua Guofeng was eventually forced to make self-criticism for this statement, and it was the fact that he refused to abandon completely this standpoint that caused his removal as chairman.

I want this to be said right now. For it is not enough to write that this book is a report with misgivings. The term report has often been misinterpreted. It is as though there had been reports that were direct slices of raw reality, that could have been placed on the desk for examination. But every report has an author, and it is his viewpoint that determines what he chooses to see. In this case, it is I, with my assumptions, who is observing a Chinese reality. This does not mean that I distort what I see, only that I have never made the naturalist mistake (Zola!) of shutting one's eyes to the fact that standpoint structures observation. The reader should not have to wonder about my basic standpoint. I see the people of Liu Lin and listen to them; I do both, convinced that it is the people who are the driving force in history, that it is in such villages as Liu Lin, not in the Great Hall of the People in Peking, where China's fate is determined. I have never thought of the world as a chessboard where the great play and make their pawn sacrifices, moving their pieces about as they choose.

Yet, this is, at the same time, a report. I have sought to report as accurately as possible what people have said. I have followed my notes. But I have left out what I consider repetition. I have given the material structure. I have chosen this form in order to allow the reader to maintain some distance from me and to draw his own conclusions. The report, as a literary genre, allows for distance and one's own viewpoint.

Yet, this report also reflects my misgivings. I try to indicate where I do not think myself capable of coming to a conclusion and where I feel I can make a judgment. My doubts, however, are not just limited to the text, they are doubts concerning developments in China. I feel that I have shown forces opposing one another and, in that way, various possible lines of development. Experience has taught me that many readers would like to be presented with an unequivocal picture. They want an answer. I am unequivocal when it comes to laying out my premises, but the report I structure is not —must not be—unequivocal. Personally, I see various possibilities. Perhaps I do not see all the potentialities present in the text. I have intentionally fashioned this book so that the reader himself must accept his responsibility for observation.

There are other ways of looking at China. Yesterday, here by the Mediterranean, I saw on television another way of portraying China. There was an official French state visit to Peking of members of parliament from various political parties. They had top-level discussions. There were also banquets and receptions and a tour for the visiting French journalists. I watched the program of that visit. It showed a new China. The various politicians were interviewed and they were all in agreement: the new policies of recent years have been beneficial to China.

(On the news I have also seen how the general secretary of the French Communist Party, Georges Marchais, has paid his respects before the embalmed corpse of Mao Zedong, and I have heard him speak of the merits and mistakes made by the deceased. It amuses me. Mao Zedong would have slapped his knee, laughed, and said: "Stick it up your ass! Some comrade! A man who has made a career in the revolution by never making revolution, who became the patriot by voluntarily working for the occupation forces, and who made a career in the Party by kissing the asses of those above him while stepping on those below—now he makes a fuss over the corpse!")

The program shows department stores and consumer goods piled on overflowing counters, as well as a peasant household with an iron bed. The bed has mattresses, and in the peasant's home there are cupboards, armchairs, and a television.

I am not criticizing the French journalists. They have reported a diplomatic visit within the limits of protocol. However, I believe they share the common error of judgment that holds that it is the cities that are of most interest and that it is the number of television sets in rich peasant homes that indicates progress.

Yet, if tomorrow China were to be struck by a series of tremendous catastrophes causing her coastal metropolises to fall into the sea and her inland cities to be devastated, China would live on and continue to develop. For China is not a small throng of several tens of millions of intellectuals and government officials, nor even 100 million or so city dwellers, but rather a vast majority of poor, hard-working peasants. China is the 800 million or so *old hundred names* out in the countryside. With their grain deliveries, their taxes, and their labor they bear the population of the cities, the whole state and its administrative apparatus, on their shoulders, today as in the past. They support the intellectuals and the city dwellers. China is a poor country of peasants in the third world.

Following the mighty peasant revolution that Mao Zedong led to a partial political victory, this traditional pattern began to change and the majority learned to make real demands for security, health, education, and a decent life. They also learned that the emperor could be "thrown from his horse." If the 800 million or so who are still poor are not soon able to see their demands met, if the revolutionary authorities prove to be of the same sort that previous victorious peasant war leaders always turned into, China may collapse.

If that should happen, no decisions taken at a plenum meeting, no matter how unanimous, will help.

The future is not predetermined. A world of equals—call it socialism—is a possibility. But an elitist, hierarchic, genocidal fascism is also a possibility. Its leaders may call themselves communists, liberals, or God fearers—the labels make no difference. In either event, the arts and sciences will evolve. The notion that aesthetic beauty and scientific progress are incompatible with genocide, oppression, and widespread corruption is a fallacy. The briefest visit to a museum will suffice to show that, unfortunately, even knives meant for human sacrifice are beautiful. One should not allow oneself to be deceived by art. Nor by science.

We are also faced with a new possibility. One that as yet only dimly looms. The practice of genocide may become rational. Its perpetration may become perfectly respectable. There are too many poor people. The world is said to be overpopulated. People in the rich countries and the wealthy in the poor nations are agreeing that it is the number of poor people that is the cause of all evil. And out of the policy of population control there grows an increasingly active policy of population reduction. The silent collusion with which the rulers of our countries (and not just ours) look on while the Soviet leaders do away with the Afghanis is not just the same silent agreement with which they looked on while the sultan annihilated the Armenians and Hitler the Jews. This may be the beginning of a new era of accord. There are so many Chinese, and they are just becoming more and more, and . . . As the Indian official in Orissa said: "The wretched poor people live like pigs in their holes. They suffer."

Premises

A time may come when the rich assist the redundant majority into a better world.

Or it would be more correct to say: A time may come when the poor masses are faced with the alternative of being exterminated or of rising up against this whole world of atrocity.

Not yet . . . but soon perhaps.

What is now happening in China may be of great, perhaps decisive, importance. If once again a wide chasm grows between the ruling upper class in the cities and an increasingly poor, increasingly numerous lower class hungry in the countryside, I believe that we are heading toward the time of large-scale genocide.

However, the questions stand unanswered; the answers have as yet to unfold. It is in Liu Lin that I try to feel my way toward them through conversations and discussions with people I have known a long time and for whom I have a deep respect. For it is there, in the countryside of China, that the future will be decided. More important than any leader—more important even than Mao Zedong —will be how *the old hundred names* react and which policies they choose to follow.

This report is related to what I previously wrote on the subject of Liu Lin and should be read in that context. It was in August 1962 that I first came to Liu Lin Brigade. I went back there in September 1982. During my first stay in Liu Lin there began the party struggle that in time would develop into the Cultural Revolution and Mao Zedong's warning: "Never forget the class struggle!"

Now, twenty years later, during my stay in Liu Lin, the party congress whose task it is to put out the fire once and for all is taking place. In the interval I have visited Liu Lin on several occasions: during the Cultural Revolution in 1969, during the campaign against "bourgeois right" in 1975, and during the last great learn-from-Dazhai campaign in 1978.

In this final report from Liu Lin I include certain discussions with advocates of various political lines in regard to Chinese agricultural policy and policy in general as well as conversations held in a district where present policy is being put into practice and being developed in a way different from Liu Lin.

But I begin with a text I wrote in the autumn of 1978. It has not previously been published. I wrote it as a sound track to a television film on Liu Lin. This is what I considered to be a correct picture of Liu Lin at that time. Today the picture is different. Policy has changed. The way it will change in the future depends on the conflicts of today.

I am grateful for the opportunity of visiting Liu Lin again. I had no conflicts with those friends from the Chinese People's Association for Friendship with Foreign Countries who accompanied and assisted me. They knew my basic outlook. We did not need to discuss it. They made efforts so that I might find the answers to the questions I posed.

1978: THE OLD HUNDRED NAMES, LIU LIN BRIGADE

Those now deciding China's future are not a handful of leaders around some table in Peking. When it comes right down to it, those who will determine the country's development are the old hundred names.

The old hundred names are all these Wangs and Lis and Zhangs and Gaos and so on who make up China's population. It is their labor that has built China. And it is the old hundred names who will determine whether Mao Zedong and Zhou Enlai's great plans for China's modernization will be realized or whether they will remain phrases and projections on a piece of paper.

Liu Lin production brigade up in the loess country of northern Shaanxi embraces 204 households living in four villages. All in all, the brigade comprises 1,005 people. What happens—or does not happen—now in Liu Lin and in all the brigades across the Chinese countryside, where the hundreds of millions of peasants labor—this is what is decisive.

It is a summer's day in Liu Lin. A workday has begun. But these young people were not born in Liu Lin. They have come here from the cities. They are youth who have finished school. Most of them will leave the brigade in the future. Some of them perhaps will go on with their studies. Others will work in factories or shops. Some perhaps will be recruited into the People's Liberation Army.

There used to be an insurmountable barrier in China between the youth studying to become officials and the common people who dug the earth and carried containers of night soil and toiled with heavy work and sweated and got calluses on their hands and coarse, sunburned skin. The youth of the cities had often never seen anything else of their country than their own city's streets and alleyways

11

and—if they were lucky and lived in this century—its parks and university. It was essential to demolish this barrier.

Since the 1950s students have come from the cities to the villages in order to work in agriculture and to gain an understanding of Chinese reality. In 1978 twelve young people came to Liu Lin. They were to stay a few years. They were also supposed to learn how to get along away from their families, to be independent and to take care of themselves and become adults. They live together in one of the newly built row of houses. The state pays the brigade for taking care of them and for putting them to work. Their ignorance and inexperience during the first year or so is such that they are not even able to produce enough by their own labor to fill their bellies. But they learn.

They also teach their own experiences gained in the cities. There are now day-care centers in Liu Lin. This is new, established just a few years ago. It was the youth from the cities who pushed for this project. They showed that day-care centers were possible, they convinced the parents, and they built up the day-care centers with help from the brigade's leadership.

If it proves possible to realize the great plans for China's modernization, these playing children in Liu Lin will live their adult lives in a developed, high-tech, socialist country. One might say that it is for the sake of these children that people in China have toiled and striven and done without through wars and revolution and long years of dogged development. They are, as Mao said, like the rising sun. They are the future. Today all children attend school. Upon graduating from Liu Lin's school, some of them go on to higher studies and become new intellectuals.

Liu Lin lies in the northern part of Shaanxi. It lies in a barren landscape. The loess plateau is scarred by deep ravines. The hills are covered with scraggly bushes. Eroded precipices gape like open wounds.

The yellow loess soil is rich. It can nourish good harvests. But it is unable to absorb water. When the rains come, the water eats muddy furrows into the ground. Each furrow cuts through the soil, slowly growing into a ravine.

1978: *The Old Hundred Names, Liu Lin Brigade*

The climate here is intemperate. Crop failures are a common occurrence. Drought, frost, and hail constitute the everpresent threats. Over a period of three years one may expect one good harvest, one bad, and one middling.

Here in northern Shaanxi the peasantry have often risen in revolt. This is a revolutionary part of the country. It was from this region that the peasant hordes who crushed the Ming dynasty in the seventeenth century came. One hundred years ago the peasants here rose up in the great Muslim war. When the imperial troops finally succeeded in putting down the uprising, more than two thirds of the population was dead.

This is a province of famine and starvation. In 1931 the Nanjing government estimated that 2 million people had starved to death in the province in the great famine then plaguing the region. Thousands of villages stood deserted. Four million people had been sold into slavery. In the early 1930s the peasants of northern Shaanxi drove off the landowners and tax collectors and established their own soviet republic and their own red army under the command of the legendary Li Qitan. It was to this base area that Mao Zedong led China's Red Worker and Peasant Army after the Long March. It was here he established his headquarters during the anti-Japanese war, and it was from here the struggle was initiated that eventually culminated in the Chinese People's Liberation Army's victory throughout the country.

In the civil war following the defeat of Japan, the village was looted and destroyed when KMT forces captured Yanan. It has taken thirty years of hard work, after the ravages of the war years, to build up the central village, with its main street and rows of new tunnel-vaulted houses.

As recently as the beginning of the 1960s, most of the families lived in stone grottoes excavated into the hills. They were warm in the winter and cool in the summer. In those days it was a great step forward that the people had something to eat and any shelter at all.

Toward the middle of the 1960s tractors came into sporadic use. Liu Lin used to borrow them from the tractor station. During the Cultural Revolution large-scale investment programs were car-

13

ried out by means of mass campaigns that terraced the hillsides and leveled the fields. Yields rose and it became possible to perceive the beginnings of a certain prosperity.

There have now been thirty years of peace. Through cooperative effort and hard work the harvests have grown. Step by step the collective has been expanded. Those who were skeptical of collectivization have since been won over for new reforms. Liu Lin Brigade in Liu Lin People's Commune has achieved a certain degree of success.

No one starves. Generations of poor peasants have dreamed of the time when common people can eat their fill every day and still be able to invite their relatives, friends, and neighbors to an occasional feast. It is not unheard of nowadays that common people eat gentry food several times a year. This has been of fundamental importance politically. The revolution kept its promise.

The collective is strong and cooperation makes things easier for everyone. The collective was able to set up a mill and the work of the women thus became lighter. But the mill, too, was first and foremost a political issue. Women's liberation has been a key issue throughout the revolution. The new marriage laws instituted after liberation were a step forward. They acknowledged as legal only those marriages voluntarily entered into by adults. But it was the new collective, electric-powered mill that liberated the women from their heaviest household chores, and it was the day-care centers that made the liberation of the women possible.

Utilizing its own raw materials, the collective manufactures noodles. The making of noodles is an ancient tradition. It was from here in northwestern China that the art of noodle making was carried to Europe by medieval travelers. Liu Lin now manufactures noodles not just to meet its own needs. Noodles from Liu Lin are sold in the shops of Yanan. They provide cash income.

The waste products from the manufacture of noodles go to feed the pigs. The collective is responsible for pig breeding. It is the old peasants who take care of the pigs. This is not heavy labor, as is plowing up on the hillsides. Middle-aged intellectuals, in Liu Lin for reschooling, were also able to work with the pigs even though they were not capable of normal farm labor. Pig breeding is a

14

communal concern. Each household then buys the piglets cheap and raises them on the family's garbage. The meat they do not consume themselves is sold to the cities. The private market plays an important role in the family's economy, as does the private plot.

Through cooperative effort it has also been possible to develop health-care services. Step by step the major reforms have been carried out. Campaigns for proper latrines and clean drinking water. Campaigns for infant hygiene and fly extermination. Soon after the people's commune reform of 1958 work began on a collective health-care service in Liu Lin. Now (since the late 1960s) the collective health-care system covers all brigade members. One might call it a health insurance system. There are barefoot doctors in each workteam. These are medical personnel who, through regular continuation courses, have been trained to be able to care for increasingly complicated cases. The brigade also has its own cottage hospital.

This achievement—the successful common effort by the people of China in providing all with basic security and the right to medical care when needed—is almost as vitally important as being able to guarantee food on the table.

In Liu Lin, as in all of China, Western medicine as well as herb medicines and traditional Chinese medicines are used. All that is harmful has been discarded and all that is useful has been utilized. The schoolchildren pick medicinal herbs in the hills, and many medicines are prepared by the brigade's own medical personnel.

All the children are vaccinated. These vaccines are supplied to the brigade by the people's commune; they come from the large, state pharmaceutical factories. If someone comes down with an illness so serious that it cannot be cured in the brigade or the people's commune, the patient is sent to specialists in Yanan or Xian or—if necessary—Peking or Shanghai.

Much of what the older generation of peasant-revolutionaries had hoped for during the 1930s and 1940s has been achieved. But most of them, such as Mao Keye or the Old Secretary Li Youhua, are already dead, while Old Secretary Li's successor has himself already been replaced by a successor.

Yet the economic foundation is still a backward, low-yielding agricultural system. There was, as Mao Zedong said, only one way out of this: the mechanization and modernization of agriculture. The peasant-revolutionary Mao Keye's son had moved to the city. He had become a worker and an electrician. He was a party member. In 1964 the party urged him to return to the village and take up the struggle for mechanization. He became a driving force, both in the technological revolution at the village level and in the Cultural Revolution. But he accepted no official posts. Today the brigade has a proper workshop. It is a prerequisite for further development. It was Mao Keye's son, Mao Peixin, who was one of those responsible for seeing that the brigade sent some people off in 1972 to learn to weld and work a lathe. They returned after three months at a vocational school, and it was then that the workshop really got going. In 1975 the next major step was taken. It was then the brigade began to produce its own spare parts. Today the workshop produces sprinkler systems for Liu Lin as well as for other brigades. By 1980 the brigade will be able to manufacture its own sowing machines, plows, harvesters, and pumping stations. By 1990 each workteam is to have its own proper workshop.

This dam construction is a common effort on the part of several brigades. It is a project for the entire Liu Lin People's Commune. The dam will provide Liu Lin and other brigades with water during the dry season. In addition, the dam will create new arable land. But this dam project also forms a part of a far larger plan than that of the people's commune or even of the province. With help from the dam, land terracing, and tree planting, erosion is being fought. This work has been going on in the Yellow River area for almost a generation. In another generation man will have triumphed over nature. China will then have been completely transformed.

The vast water regulation projects along the Yellow River are world famous. But they are not the decisive factor. They only provide temporary relief. Then they, too, will silt up again. What is really decisive is what brigades such as Liu Lin are able to accomplish. It is here in the small, narrow valleys, where the rains carve ravines into the loess earth, that it will be decided if China will be able to defeat erosion and, with that, the silting up and the flood catastrophes. If China were forced to choose between the large, ultramodern, enormously expensive (and therefore famous) projects and the small projects out among the workteams and brigades, it would be the small, seemingly insignificant rather than the large, world-renowned projects that had to be carried out, no matter what, if China were to survive.

There are many city youth working on this project. Most of them remain in the countryside only a few years. But it is here, and not in Shanghai, that they are learning to understand China's real problems. Gigantic plans such as the Yellow River Project can be drawn up on paper, but they are realized through the hard toil of the working people. All these young people are being transformed by this experience. At the same time, they are also transforming the countryside. Some of them choose to remain here the rest of their lives. One of these is Li Lin, an officer's daughter who once worked as army telephone operator in Lanzhou.

As recently as the early 1960s, the brigade cleared new land up on the hillsides and increased the land planted in wheat. Now trees are being planted on what had once been fields. Wheat acreage has decreased. This means that policy has changed. But the fact that policy has changed does not mean that the aim and direction have changed. Grain production is increasing because a more profitable method is being pursued.

On the wall of the brigade's meeting room there hangs a painting. It was done by some young people from the city. It shows how Liu Lin will look in a few years, when the plans have been carried out. Fruit trees will grow on all the hillsides. All the houses will be new. There will be irrigation ponds full of fish. And the ravines will have been transformed into fertile fields where the newest varieties of wheat will grow.

This is a great plan and a huge task. Work has been going on now since 1975, and already results are beginning to show. The gullies are to be filled up, the hills leveled out. The chopped-up landscape is to be transformed into one that is more erosion-resistant, with broad, fertile valleys whose fields are well-suited to cultivation by tractors. The rain will be collected in reservoirs and the runoff carefully regulated. The higher hills will be planted in groves of trees. The work is carried out both by advanced technique, such as the use of water cannon to wash down the loess soil, and by the traditional hoe and shovel. The country is being dug over.

It is a scientific- and technology-oriented generation of farmers that is now taking over in Liu Lin. They try out new political methods. The brigade's current chairman is Li Qisheng. He grew up here in the village during Li Youhua's term in office. Later he became a leader and a revolutionary Red Guard in Yanan during the Cultural Revolution, and as such he returned to Liu Lin to work as a teacher. He was then chosen to be responsible for production.

New methods of production have now been introduced. Agriculture is to be run along scientific, rational lines. The brigade's representatives come back from meetings and conferences in Yanan, bringing with them new tips and improved methods of pest control —less poisonous and more effective.

Liu Lin Brigade has also set up its own laboratory. This became necessary, since the new methods call for analysis and research. Plain experience and good intentions are no longer enough. This new laboratory also became possible due to the arrival of educated youth from the cities. The young people who work in the brigade's laboratory have also studied agricultural engineering.

But the leader of this operation is Luo Hanhong. It is he who holds the responsibility. Twenty years ago he was a greedily reading peasant boy. Even then he was passionately interested in modernization and spoke of the future when the village would have electricity. Later he became the brigade bookkeeper. In 1975 he was chosen operative leader of the brigade's experimental division. It is not enough to have a highly educated intelligentsia in the cities. It is, as Chairman Hua Guofeng said at the national conference on science in March 1978, the scientific and cultural level of the entire Chinese nation that must be raised.

Two years ago Luo Hanhong and his experimental group challenged the veteran peasants. There had been heated debate over the new agricultural methods. This was to be the conclusive contest as to which policy was best suited for Liu Lin. The experimental group and the skeptical peasants were each given a field bordering the other and were allowed to choose their own farming methods. The experimental group got a much higher yield with the new scientific methods. The old peasants then gave up their resistance to the new techniques. The new methods have now been introduced throughout the brigade.

Since 1975 Luo Hanhong and his experimental group have been working in cooperation with the Shaanxi Agricultural Engineering Institute in order to develop through radiation a more frost-resistant variety of millet for northern Shaanxi.

It is on a higher-yielding agriculture in brigades such as Liu Lin that China's future is being built. If yields do not increase, China will not succeed in carrying out her plans. But rising yields must also signify a higher standard of living for the peasants. One of Mao Zedong's main criticisms of Soviet economic policy was that it meant an exploitation and bleeding of the peasantry.

For several years now there have been plans in Liu Lin Brigade to provide all households with new, permanent dwellings. This goal has almost been reached. All that remains is a few more winters' work. The dwellings are sometimes called grottoes. This is incorrect. They are tunnel-vaulted houses with a very thick layer of earth as insulation. They are sturdily built. The houses also have the advantage of being cool in the summer and easily heated in winter.

The commune's main store is now located in Liu Lin. It serves many brigades. There are also smaller shops in the various villages. An effort is being made to continually increase the availability of consumer goods in the rural areas. Prices are kept constant. This is a cornerstone of economic policy. The low standard of living must be raised radically and swiftly, but without inflation.

The price the state pays for agricultural commodities is kept high to allow the collectives to increase their revenues in a planned way. This in turn permits them to make investments and expand production and so provide their members with higher earnings. Liu Lin is not one of the best brigades. But neither is it one of the worst. There are brigades whose production has stagnated, where people have such a hard time that they are close to hunger. To overcome this situation is one of the fundamental political problems facing China.

Liu Lin has enjoyed political stability for a long period. So too have the majority of Chinese brigades. Those struggles that have taken place have been over concrete issues concerning the aim and direction of production and investment plans, questions as to what portion of brigade revenues should go to consumption, what percentage of this consumption should be spent on social services, and what percentage should be directly linked to work performance. Criticism has often been voiced. But afterward, those in positions of responsibility have been allowed to stay on.

When the supervisory committee meets to report and debate prior to the summer harvest, the discussion keeps to the facts.

The old peasant-revolutionaries had taken part in the struggles of the 1930s and helped chase off the landowners and tax collectors. Their younger brothers fought against the Japanese. Their sons took part in the guerrilla warfare against the KMT troops during the occupation of 1947. Now, their grandchildren, both girls and boys, belong to the people's militia, the armed militia.

The threat of war is a real one for the people of Liu Lin. The people's militia drills home defense. In case of war, its task is to defend the immediate surrounding areas in cooperation with the People's Liberation Army. If the enemy advances and occupies the home district, the people's militia is to form the nucleus for the guerrilla struggle. It should be able to mobilize at the shortest possible notice, in the event of a surprise attack or sudden landing of airborne troops.

As evening comes, the youth association's amateur theater ensemble is rehearsing down by the brigade office. The piece is about a drama-loving old carpenter who goes to the village to see a play his son-in-law is producing. But the play is about the carpenter himself. It criticizes him for having capitalist ideas and for going around the countryside doing odd jobs instead of working for the brigade. Now he laments before his daughter.

The old carpenter is played by the son of Mao Peixin, the electrician and truck driver, who was the son of Mao Keye, the peasant-revolutionary. He himself is one of the leading members of the people's militia. He is known for his voice and acting talent.

Many of the older people are content with things as they are now. They have accomplished what they once set out to do. They feel no great need to develop the brigade's agriculture from the ox-

and-cart level to that of the tractor and sprinkler system. They do not see the necessity of it and they are not dissatisfied with what has already been achieved. But most of the younger people are impatient. Several of them are now in the vanguard of the effort to modernize agriculture. China needs these impatient youths in Liu Lin and the rest of the country in order to be able to transform agriculture and swiftly raise crop yields. Impatience is a motor.

The isolation of the village is a thing of the past. Newspapers and the radio do their work. The party's slogans are spread by the various mass organizations. Television has now come to Liu Lin. As almost everywhere else in China, the sets are owned collectively. People gather in front of the television to watch movies. The television is purposely used to spread impatience and to urge the old, poor village to move forward and develop.

Far into the night the youth from the cities pore over their textbooks. They are preparing to take the university entrance examinations. China has a great lack of educated people for this new Long March that is to carry the old hundred names—all of China's people—up out of poverty.

AT ISSUE

The description of Liu Lin in the foregoing broadcast-narration from 1978 had a positive tone. That is the way I saw the brigade. One might say that what I described had more than fortuitous similarities to a scene depicting the Swedish welfare state of the 1930s or 1940s, with its newly built cooperative shop designed by the Co-op's own architect firm in the middle of the village and a People's Palace with its study-circle rooms and stage for the local amateur theater ensemble. The Old Secretary Feng moves through the text like some Swedish municipal honcho. Proud, yet without exaggeration, he tells of plans for the future. There will be the new tract of terraced houses and there will be new industries.

Yes, there was so much in Liu Lin that made me glad then. Not just that the brigade's economy was developing and that production was rising and that the people were living many times better than they had in the early 1960s. Through their own efforts the brigade had built a workshop and the workshop had begun to change from a repair facility into a small industry. Fourteen years after Mao Peixin was sent back to the village to work as a Communist for technological modernization, the village not only had electricity and tractors but had itself begun to manufacture sprinkler systems and talk of its plans for the future with obvious pride.

When officious cadres from Peking tried to button Mao Peixin's shirt when he was to be filmed, he shooed them away. He was a worker and proud of it. He did not want to look like an office worker and did not play coy when interviewed.

It was the village's own young people who performed amateur pieces they had written themselves. In the early 1960s there had already existed amateur theater, and now this tradition was being carried on by a new generation. And these amateur playlets were political agitation pieces directly adapted to the conditions and debates then present in the brigade.

The bright youth of 1962 had now grown to be adults, and it

was they who pushed forward the modernization they had once spoken of. Luo Hanhong's experimental group, whose first discussion I had heard in 1975, had now been able to prove to the skeptical older peasants that the new farming methods were superior to the old. And the group had succeeded in this by utilizing the city youth who had been sent out to the countryside. It was the brigade's own members, the wise Feng and the clever Luo Hanhong, who held the leadership, but they made use of the knowledge and skill of the city youth and directed their efforts so that their learning became useful.

The youth from the cities were not so bombastically romantic as they had once been during the Cultural Revolution. Many of them made great contributions. Take, for example, the girls who some years earlier had succeeded in opening day-care centers for the children. That meant a great deal for women's liberation in Liu Lin. But it meant even more for the children. The superior scholastic results generally obtained by city children were largely due to the extra school years they received in day-care centers. It was there they learned to read and to work together. It was there they learned the basics. Day-care centers were essential if the gap between city and countryside was to be bridged.

The large-scale investment plans meant to transform the brigade within a few years were sound. They did not call for sacrifices as heavy as during the Cultural Revolution, when consumption was cut back in favor of investment (which now gave a manifold return and which had laid the foundation for today's relative prosperity). The proportion of investment to consumption seemed reasonable. It was obvious that the inhabitants of Liu Lin, and especially the youth, realized the necessity of digging in order to assure future harvests. They were, after all, peasants. But, in addition, these plans were of the utmost importance to China as a whole, and a swift realization of these plans in Liu Lin and thousands of other brigades was essential so that the great rivers would not silt up and, in the coming decades and centuries, not regularly cause huge catastrophes in the lowlands.

No direct taxes were levied on the members of Liu Lin Brigade, but the collective used a portion of its earnings for social security, health care, and culture. The remainder was shared out according to work contribution. One might say that the portion deducted for public spending in Liu Lin corresponded to the taxes used to finance social welfare programs in such countries as Sweden. However, this is not quite accurate. The economic systems of our countries are totally different. Nonetheless, it is this question—What percentage of labor earnings should be paid directly to the worker for his labor and what percentage withheld for social spending and welfare programs—that is the most-debated political issue among normal working people in Liu Lin, as well as in Flint, Michigan.

The ratio between the share used for social spending and that which could be used directly for private consumption had been altered several times. Following a period of miscalculation in autumn 1975, when the part to be spent on social programs increased so much that, as Feng had said in 1978, many had lost the will to work, the situation in Liu Lin in 1978 was back to what it had been in the middle of the 1970s. Each member was covered by a basic insurance, regardless of age or health, and, in addition, received his direct and personal income for the work performed.

The equivalent issue in Sweden would be discussed in such terms as *tax burden* and *tax strain*. But, as in Sweden, there was, to my knowledge, no one in Liu Lin who suggested that the public sector should be completely abolished. At issue were minor adjustments of the ratio between public and private consumption, as well as that between investment and consumption.

Thus, there were controversies and problems in Liu Lin, but it was (and still is) my opinion that they were not the kind that could lead to a change of course. There were just no forces pushing for such a change in Liu Lin.

Four years later, the situation is different. Liu Lin now forms a part of a suburb. Even back in the 1960s the city had been creeping closer. In the middle of the 1970s a decision had been made to build a railway to Yanan, and the track was to run through the valley, where the station would eventually also be built. This would mean that Liu Lin would lose good farmland. But the brigade prepared to compensate this loss by construction work up in the ravines where the new fields had been created. Now, in 1982, no one knows when the railroad will be built. But the city keeps expanding. It has leaped the river and spread out across arable land. The large new housing projects push out through what was once Seven Mile Village, and the new trunk road cuts across the fields and old settlements. Even before the railroad is built, Liu Lin will have lost the good arable land down in the valley.

Beyond Liu Lin, farther up the valley, lie three new factories. Thick smoke from the expanded cement factory covers Liu Lin. People cough.

"Many suffer bronchial infections now that the cement factory has been enlarged," says Doctor Wang Youneng. "It is particularly hard on the children."

While the brigade is finding itself being engulfed by the city, which twenty years earlier lay so far away, the people's commune is in the process of building out over the brigade's land. The commune administration has had to leave its small old offices in Seven Mile Village, where the city's suburbs have stretched in advance of the railroad. Instead, the commune has built large administration facilities on what used to be fields, once prepared for tractor cultivation.

The brigade workshop has moved to new premises, but it is said that the enterprise is no longer a profitable affair. Its workers are penalized by wage deductions. It no longer manufactures sprinkler systems. Instead it produces iron beds for the market. The great plans from 1978 will not be realized. Mao Peixin no longer works in Liu Lin; he has become a truck driver for the commune.

The experimental group and its laboratory have ceased to function, although the new methods once tested are now in general use. The youth from the cities are gone. The day-care centers are closed. The new party secretary at the school looks at me and says, "It is intelligence that determines who goes on to higher studies. So there won't be so many children from the countryside."

Not even Li Lin, who was a member of the brigade supervisory committee and who had decided to stay for the rest of her life, who had reportedly fallen in love and therefore did not want to leave— not even she is still here.

And the great plans for erosion control have not been carried out. Less is invested and more privately consumed. When it rains, the water cuts furrows in the earth and the yellow silt of the loess soil runs off down toward the rivers.

At New Year the health insurance society was abolished. Health care would have to cover its own costs.

"But the people objected and we health-care workers felt that the decision was wrong," said Wang Youneng. "One cannot make hygiene campaigns, vaccination drives, and health care into profit-making enterprises. The criticism of the people, and our own, grew so strong that they were forced to reverse their decision to do away with the health insurance society. It will go on working as in the past."

As for the construction of private tunnel-vaulted houses, goals have been met, perhaps surpassed. Some families have enjoyed a rise in living standards. They bicycle into the city to sell their produce at the market and to shop in the stores. The main store in Liu Lin has closed down. It is no longer needed now that the city has come so close. For those unable to get into the city there is a small shop stocking the most essential household items.

At six in the morning the loudspeakers around the commune's large administrative center begin to blare out over the brigade. The air is thick and people cough and spit. In the fields work has long been in progress.

I have serious misgivings as to the way things are developing. It seems ominous to me. I fill my notebooks with questions I cannot answer. What seems most alarming is that this time, unlike the situation even during the Cultural Revolution, I do not see that the initiative for these changes has come from the inhabitants of Liu Lin themselves. They follow along unwillingly. But the initiative is not in their hands.

(WORKERS OF THE WORLD), ENRICH YOURSELVES!

In Peking, Director Qin Qiming, assistant head of the Department of Research for People's Communes, and Zhang Houyi, research assistant at the same institute, describe the new agricultural policies.

"In recent years, grain production, as well as other agricultural production, has increased. The grain harvest for 1978 was 304.75 million tons. In 1981, it rose to 325.02 million tons, or an increase of 6.7 percent. As for such crops as cotton, oil-yielding plants, and sugar, the increases were even greater. Cotton production went up from 2.17 million tons to 2.97 million tons, a 37-percent increase. The harvest of oil-yielding crops rose from 5.22 million tons to 10.21 million tons, an increase of 95.6 percent. Sugarcane production rose from 21.12 million tons to 29.67 million tons, a 40.5-percent rise. Sugar beets went from 2.70 million tons to 6.36 million tons, an increase of 135.4 percent. These are just a few examples to illustrate our claim that grain production, as well as other agricultural production, has increased.

"The explanation for this change is to be found in the decisions taken by the third plenum meeting of China's Communist Party's Eleventh Central Committee, which took place from the eighteenth to the twenty-second of December 1978. This meeting decided on a thoroughgoing change of policy and corrected the "leftist" errors committed prior to, and during, the so-called Cultural Revolution. Thus ceased the vacillation that had characterized party policy ever since the fall of the Gang of Four, in October 1976. The meeting adopted a decision of principle concerning political and economic strategy, a decision that marked a turning point in the history of New China."

(It was at this meeting that the policy of holding to Chairman Mao's line and following Chairman Mao's directives as a

guiding principle for party work was declared to be erroneous; the meeting decided that the "two whatevers" were to be combated. Class struggle was no longer to be taken as the main link; this was not suitable to conditions in a socialist society. Instead, it was socialist modernization that was on the agenda.)

"Let us look, then, at the situation in the Chinese countryside before the Eleventh Central Committee rectified party policy at its third plenum. The situation was the following:

"1. Production management was carried out blindly. This was because the political and economic decision-making functions were in the hands of the same people. Decisions pertaining to production were made by administrative fiat, and not on relevant grounds. The leadership made too many decisions. When to sow or to harvest was decided by the party committee. One decision was made for the entire district, and the masses had absolutely nothing to say.

"2. The work was done collectively. At a given order, everyone had to go into the fields. Everyone had the same work to do. No one had any specific responsibility for anything. The result was poor work; quality was low and so was production.

"3. Distribution was egalitarian. As we say, everyone ate from the same pot. Egalitarianism was perhaps the most serious problem we faced. Everybody had approximately the same standard of living. The good workers lost their zeal when they saw the shirkers eating as much as themselves. Those who were lazy were not encouraged to become diligent.

"These political errors caused China's economy to advance slowly. The country should have been able to make more progress in the agricultural sector. This was especially evident during the Cultural Revolution.

"In December 1978 the Central Committee moved to correct these errors and decided the following:

"1. Responsibility was to be introduced. Direct responsibility for the work being done well, direct responsibility for the work being done poorly. Remuneration according to work performed.
"2. The peasants' right to private plots, which had been abolished during the Cultural Revolution, was to be guaranteed and markets established where the peasants could freely sell their products."

(There had been private plots in Liu Lin even during the Cultural Revolution. I had also visited markets in various localities in China in 1975, 1976, and 1978—a half year before the Central Committee's decision. Even in the middle of the great campaign in summer 1976, the free markets flourished.)

"3. The purchase price for agricultural products paid by the state was to be increased in order to improve the economic lot of the peasantry, while, at the same time, city dwellers were to be compensated. In March 1979 the government effected this policy. The purchase price of eighteen agricultural commodities, including grain, oil-yielding plants, cotton, and hogs, was increased by an average of 25.8 percent.

"Considering the actual situation in the country, it is obvious that agricultural production must increase. Generally speaking, the situation following the third plenum of the Eleventh Central Committee shows a marked improvement.

"From 1953 to 1981 the average annual increase in grain production was 2.4 percent. Between 1978 and 1981 the increase was 2.2 percent per year. Nineteen seventy-nine was a record year, 1980 was almost a record year despite difficulties, and 1981 was better than the year before despite great natural disasters.

"Cotton production increased an average 2.9 percent from

1953 to 1981. But between 1979 and 1981, the annual increase jumped to 11 percent. Oil-yielding crops showed an annual growth of 3.1 percent between 1953 and 1981. But the annual increase was 25.1 percent for the period 1979–1981.

"And we could go on and on. We see, then, that the market crops—cotton, oil plants, sugarcane, sugar beets, tea, and so on—show rapid gains, whenever grain production has not increased at all.

"The average per-capita income in the rural area is low. But in the last few years it has risen markedly. In 1970 prices the average per-capita income was:

1976:	113 ¥
1978:	134 ¥
1979:	160 ¥
1980:	191 ¥
1981:	223 ¥

"This includes income from the collective and household income from private production and sales, as well as income stemming from family members' work in the cities (that is, what they send back to the village).

"Generally speaking, the peasants have enough to eat. But great disparity exists among various areas. Differences also exist among different households. Some are better off than others. There is nothing wrong with that; on the contrary, it's an indication of rapid all-around economic development. There is nothing wrong with some people becoming rich before the rest. In the past there were restrictions. No one was allowed to have more than this amount or that. This put a damper on the zeal to work. The strong, those with initiative, lost the will to work, and the poor sat about listlessly waiting to receive their share. Now, we are intentionally creating inequality, a disparity among individuals, as well as among various provinces and regions.

"The rich man serves as a good example for the others. Wealth is worthy of imitation. The state grows stronger. The entire national economy develops more rapidly. This is an effective policy. It forces development. Facts show that with this policy an increasing number of brigades in recent years have passed the level where per-capita annual income exceeds 300 ¥."

(When considering this question of the unequal development of China's provinces, one should remember that, as in all third world countries, it is very great. In 1981 the total per-capita product from industry and agriculture amounted to 5,558 ¥ in Shanghai, but only 473 ¥ in Sichuan. In Yunnan, Tibet, and Guizhou, it was even less. If one then compares the income of the city dweller of Shanghai with that of the peasant in the rural areas of Sichuan, northern Shaanxi, or western Gansu, the difference is still greater. Liu Lin ranks among the more successful brigades in the vicinity of Yanan. In 1981, the per-capita product there totaled 335 ¥, less than one sixteenth of the Shanghai amount!)

"In the past, we moved factories out of Shanghai into the hinterland. Now we are taking the more profitable road and allowing them to remain in the developed areas. Since December 1978, we are following the economic laws and are producing where it is cheapest. In the long run it will be worth Shanghai's while to contribute to the development of the hinterland from where it gets energy and raw materials.

"Inequality is going to increase, especially in the poor, backward areas of the country. This cannot be avoided. For example, good cadres are needed in these areas. In China, as in all countries, there exists a natural tendency for people to move to places where conditions are better. Here they cannot really move wherever they like, but the tendency is there. To counteract this, and to assure that the backward parts of the country also get good cadres, there should be a policy that encourages the intellectuals to remain there. If they are treated well and are given a relatively high living standard, they are willing to stay and work in the hinterland. And yet this also means that inequality will be the most extreme in just these areas that are the very poorest. An extra lot is needed to make the intellectuals want to stay there.

"Now we're not talking about truck drivers or such workers. They are well off in any case. What we're talking about are the essential technical and administrative cadres who otherwise would move down toward the coastal cities.

"These new policies will be in effect for a long time to come. There are not going to be any sudden changes. The peasants can count on the stability of the party's present course. Many peasants have expressed concern over party policy, but no changes are going to be made. And:

"1.   China will continue on the road to socialism. There will be no change in this course.

"2.   The means of production will not become private property.

"3.   The policy of assigned responsibility will remain in effect for a very long time to come.

"4.   The interests of the state, as well as those of the collective and the individual, have been taken into consideration.

"In the following areas, particular consideration will be shown when carrying out these new policies:

"1.   The old revolutionary bases and wartime base areas,

"2.   Mountain areas,

"3.   Minority areas, and

"4.   Remote areas and border regions.

"The government emphasizes the need for planning, and in areas where the peasants have preferred to produce for the free market to the point where grain production has suffered, steps will naturally have to be taken. Planning is there so that imbalances do not arise. This is achieved by providing the peasants with a material interest in the production of grain. But our policy of importing grain will continue for a long time, since it is profitable. It allows us to make use of the land in the best possible manner. We will also continue with our policy of gradually altering eating habits, encouraging people to switch to eating rice, thereby permitting the exportation of rice. Rice, as you know, provides good export income. In the past, wheat acreage was increased in a way harmful to the production of more lucrative grains. Now we cultivate the most profitable grain. We export whatever brings in a good income and import wheat.

"The system of assigned responsibility can be effected in many different ways. Depending on local conditions, the system is organized so that the responsibility rests either on an entire workteam or on an individual household. In some instances this means that the collective can still pay for teachers and health care, while in others these welfare systems have been abolished. However, the fundamental guarantees for families made up of invalids, the sick, or elderly lacking relatives able to care for them, as well as for families with sons in the People's Liberation Army, should be assured through contracts between the aid recipients and the local collective."

(Various examples of how the contract system was organized were also presented. But I was also told that I should investigate for myself. I have chosen to report how the system works as it was described to me on the spot. This way it will be clearer and easier to understand.)

SOME BACKGROUND TO THE NEW AGRICULTURAL POLICIES

"From the end of 1955 to the first months of 1956, almost all peasants were organized in socialist higher agricultural cooperatives, and their private means of production became collective property. The peasants were not happy when the promises to reimburse them for what they had handed over to the collective was never kept.

"In 1957 peasants in certain areas began to adopt the system of assigning production quotas to each household. This, however, was quickly branded a 'spontaneous capitalist tendency' and was halted.

"To escape famine during the three years of serious economic difficulties (1959–1961), many peasants again resorted to assigning production quotas to the individual households. This time this mass movement was noticed by certain leading cadres who found the system effective in increasing production and providing the peasants with food and clothing. These cadres recommended to the Party Central Committee that the system of responsibility in agriculture be accepted. Soon afterward, this was sharply criticized as revisionism.

"Following the Eleventh Central Committee's third plenum (December 1978), which corrected the 'leftist' deviations in rural policy, quotas for agricultural production were assigned to workteams in certain areas. The peasants preferred a system of responsibility, where the quotas were given directly to the households. In those places where the local leadership, with the support of the Central Committee, tried this system, production increased.

In October 1980 the Central Committee drew up a document based on the experiences of the masses. They proposed various forms of responsibility in rural production and allowed the peasants to choose the form where the individual household was responsible. The peasants' enthusiasm for production, repressed for so many years, was finally unleashed."

Du Runsheng, remarks made during a group discussion at the Twelfth Party Congress

A MODEL DISTRICT

Fengyang District in Anhui Province now serves as a model. One might say that, in regard to agricultural policy of the 1980s, it has been given the role that Dazhai once held for Mao Zedong's agricultural policies: that of the good example.

This used to be a poor district. This was a beggar district. Nine years out of ten there was a bad harvest. It was here in this district that the system of responsibility evolved into one of individual contracts.

According to Vice-Chairman Wang Zhangtai, "The district has a population of 540,000, inhabiting forty-five peoples communes and two cities. Rice and wheat are the main crops. Cultivated acreage totals 1.2 million mu. In addition to the ancient irrigation works, we have what has been dug since liberation. At present 650,000 mu are under irrigation, and of this total there are 350,000 mu so well irrigated and ditched that they yield a good harvest regardless of the weather.

"From 1949 to 1955 agricultural production showed a satisfactory, steady development. Production rose from 99 million jin a year in 1949 to 260 million jin in 1955. Then followed a period of fluctuating results. In 1978 295 million jin were harvested, while the best year had been 1977, with 360 million jin. The district acquired a nationwide reputation for backwardness.

"Between 1949 and 1978, we were unable to supply the state with even a single jin of grain; just the opposite, the state had to supply us with 370 million jin during this period just to keep us from starving. Over the same period, the state invested 44 million ¥ in construction works, while the communes, brigades, and workteams took loans totaling 23 million ¥ to increase production. On top of all this, the state granted the district 40.5 million ¥ in emergency assistance and 11.8 million ¥ to relieve famine.

"Ninety percent of the population are peasants, and they were profoundly embarrassed over this backwardness and lack of development. Following the Eleventh Central Committee's third plenum in December 1978, we organized discussions among the peasants and found a new solution. We put into practice the system of responsibility with direct contracts between individual households and the collective. The first year this new system was in effect was 1979, when 440 million jin of grain were harvested. In 1980 we grew 502 million jin and in 1981, 642 million jin. In 1979 we were able to sell the state 89 million jin. By 1980 this amount had risen to 115 million jin and in 1981 it reached 230 million jin. This has meant great changes for the people. In 1978 the [average] per-capita income was 70 ¥, whereas in 1981 it had risen to 295 ¥. During the last three years the peasants have built 30,000 units of rooms with tile roofing, purchased 15,000 sewing machines, 16,000 bicycles, 42,000 wristwatches, and 60,000 radios. The collective economy is flourishing. The brigades have built 100 miles of all-weather roads, and of the 150 miles of high-voltage power lines put up, half have been paid for directly by the individual households and half by the state. We have built thirty movie theaters, which can also be used to put on plays. Ticket receipts cover costs.

"There are agricultural contracts and contracts for specialized households. The specialized households go in for animal breeding, poultry farming, or handicrafts, commerce, or other service occupations. But nine out of ten households are engaged in farming. The contract is drawn up between the collective and the household. It is the head of the household who signs for his entire family, including sons, daughters, and even daughters-in-law.

"Land, animals, and machines are all divided up. The land is the only thing that cannot be bought or sold. In this district there were 40,000 animals, the peasants have since bought another 20,000 head. We had 15,000 tractors, and the peasants have bought an additional 15,000.

"The land is divided among the households according to the size of the family. This division takes place after a general discussion, so that it is done fairly. The land remains the property of the collective. We have explained to the peasants that we guarantee two constants:

"1.   Collective ownership of the land will remain; land cannot be sold, bought, or leased.

"2.   The system of responsibility will remain unchanged for the foreseeable future.

"If the family splits up, if the head of the household dies, if the sons build their own households or the daughters marry, none of this has anything to do with the collective. The family may divide up its land the way it sees fit. This land, which has been distributed to a family according to its size, will not be curtailed if the number of family members decreases. This distribution stands."

(The leasing of land is not permitted, but cooperation is. Cooperation can, for example, take the form of one peasant, who successfully and skillfully grows hybrid rice on his own land, also cultivating it on another's and in return handing over a portion of the harvest to the landholder.)

"The contract is made between the workteam and the individual household. In this contract the rights and duties of the state, the collective, and the individual household are stipulated. The contract fixes the state agricultural tax. This tax is set and remains unchanged. The contract also lays down the state purchase quota. It is the responsibility of the contracting peasant to deliver this quota at a set price. If he does not have these commodities, he must purchase them on the open market. But the quotas are set in such a way that the peasant should have no difficulty in meeting his obligations. The contract also stipulates the fees the contracting peasant must hand over to the collective for the payment of cadres and other public businesses. In addition, the contract establishes the general production plan to be followed by the contracting peasant. Whatever the peasant produces that exceeds or falls outside the contract he may do with as he likes—sell it on the open market or whatever. The contract runs for one year, and, of course, the quotas are variable from year to year."

(Landownership is collective, but what, in actual fact, is

the form of ownership? The land can be inherited, retained, and, naturally, even lost [if taxes are not paid and responsibilities in conjunction with the possession of the land are not met]. And, even if the practice is called cooperation and not leasehold, land can still be turned over to others to cultivate in return for a portion of the harvest. However, land cannot be bought, sold, or mortgaged, as had previously been the case in China.

The strict contention that proprietary rights remain unchanged and are written into the constitution and laws seems to me mainly a formal truth. The real ownership-possession-utilization strikes me as being more closely related to that of old India, where the lord owned all the land but the peasants occupied and cultivated it. However, India was a feudal country, whereas China is socialist. Still, the situation is not the same as existed at the time of the land reform during liberation: the land, to be sure, is divided up among the peasants again, but today there exists no movement toward the formation of mutual-aid teams in these districts. The cooperation that does take place among various households is governed by the demands and opportunities of the market.

Consider this as a possible parallel: Handicraft production is once again unrestricted. In return for a stipulated tax and without other, unexpected levies, the craftsman may work confidently toward increasing his assets. These assets are inviolable in a socialist society, as they are the product of his own labor and have not arisen through exploitation. Since October 17, 1981, however, the craftsman has the right to employ in his workshop two wage-earning assistants, as well as five salaried apprentices—a total of seven persons. Still, the assets are considered to be a result of the craftsman's personal work contribution and not to have arisen through exploitation, and so they are inviolable. Words and reality no longer agree.)

"The cooperative health-care service has shut down. Instead, the physicians have established a collective clinic where the team of doctors itself bears the responsibility for profits and losses. The peasants pay for treatment and consultations. Regarding preventive medicine, contracts are drawn up between the collective of doctors and the state. Thus, programs are carried out against polio, malaria, adult measles, diphtheria, and encephalitis. The decision as to which measures to take and fees are made centrally. The state-employed cadres, white-collar workers, factory workers, and employees in the state retail and wholesale trades have their health care paid for by the government. Women in the rural areas are not obliged to visit a hospital, doctor, or midwife, either before or after childbirth. Of course, they can if they want to, but it costs them.

"We have 93,000 children and youth attending school. In the city, 95 percent of school-age children attend classes, whereas in the countryside the percentage is less. Some families now do not want to let their seven- or eight-year-olds go to school, since they require their labor in the fields. In 1978 there were 12,000 children attending the first grade. Later, the number dwindled to 10,000. Today it is somewhat better, as we are up to 11,000. We reckon that about 2,000 children are kept home to work. We hope that in about three years we will be back to where we were in 1978. Hopefully, the peasants will then be so well off that they will be able to afford to allow their children to attend school.

"Fifty percent of the city children go on to middle school. Of the children in the rural areas, 20 percent continue on to middle school. Government grants for education amount to 3.3 million ¥. The collective contributes 540,000 ¥. Tuition is 5 ¥ per pupil per term for elementary school, and 12 ¥ per pupil per term for middle school. The tuition is the same in the country and the city.

"In the past, we did not take family planning seriously enough. Ten years ago the birthrate was 30 per thousand. In 1976 we got it down to 23 per thousand, and by 1981 we were down to 12.5 per thousand. We think that it will be difficult to get below 10 per thousand. But we have now established a system of reward and punishment, and it is getting results. Out of 53,000 women of child-bearing age, 42,000 take steps to prevent pregnancy. These measures are: sterilization, intrauterine devices, birth-control pills, and condoms for the men. Ninety-eight percent of the sterilizations are performed on women, 2 percent on men. This is because feudal notions are still strong. The man is the head of the household, he who provides the income, he who supports the family. If anything happens to him, or if his strength should fail him, the family would be in trouble. We have tried to carry out campaigns in order to get men to agree to sterilization—it is, after all, so much easier and safer—but even when we succeeded in convincing the men, their women opposed it. The women of the family came to the clinic and dragged their men away. They were afraid the men would lose their strength.

"Between 5 and 10 percent of the women taking measures to prevent pregnancy fail in their efforts. Each spring and autumn a checkup is made, and in the event of pregnancy, an abortion is performed.

"We reward single-child families. They receive 5 ¥ per month from the collective if the child is a boy, and 6 ¥ if it is a girl. In addition, single-child families are given an extra private plot. The private plots are not included in the collective's land-distribution system. In the case of a state employee, the family is allotted extra living space. In addition, the only child is given priority in education and other matters.

"The family with two children, on the other hand, is penalized. The family must pay 5 ¥ a month for the second child. This money is used to reward the single-child families. With the third child, the fines are doubled. This policy will be in effect for a long time, until the population has become stable. At that time, it may be possible to allow families to have two children. The problem, you see, is quite serious. The increase in population is an acute problem. A few years ago we believed that by using these methods we could get down to a population growth of nine per thousand. Now we realize that we cannot achieve this goal. But we have reached twelve per thousand.

"There are, naturally, some exceptions. If the first child is retarded, the family is allowed to have a second without suffering any penalties.

"Families in difficulty, families who have lost their breadwinner, old people without relatives to support them, the sick who cannot support themselves, and families with sons serving in the People's Liberation Army—all received help and economic support from the collective. The district has a quota of 300 recruits to the PLA. We receive 50,000 applications. It is difficult to make the selection. There are now 1,050 families in the district who have one son—or, in some cases, two—in the army. These families receive an annual subsidy of 176.50 ¥ per soldier from the collective. Thus, a family with two sons in the army receives more than 300 ¥ per year from the collective.

"A contract is drawn up with the families who are in need of help. They now constitute less than 1 percent of the households. According to the contract, they receive a certain quantity of various commodities. The amount depends on individual circumstances. They can also borrow money at a low, 1.8 percent annual interest rate, to get themselves out of temporary difficulty.

"Families with only a daughter or daughters are considered as being childless when reckoning subsidies.

"We have now been living under socialism for thirty years and have learned some serious lessons. There was too much bossing and too many checkups; initiative was stifled. We also practiced an egalitarian policy in regard to distribution. The diligent and the lazy received almost equal shares. Thus, the industrious peasants were not rewarded and felt no enthusiasm for work. There was no place for talent and competence. In addition, those who did work had too many bosses over them. Various leaders went about directing the work, and they, of course, also had to be fed.

"We've now gotten rid of a third of the cadres at the brigade level. Their work is no longer needed, since the individual peasants manage their own labor and accounts. These former cadres can now farm instead.

"However, there are also negative tendencies in these developments that we have to watch out for. It will take five or ten years to solve these problems. They are the following:

"1.   Political and ideological work has become more difficult. In the past, when people labored collectively, it was possible to carry out political education and to explain

42

current policies and the problems facing the country and district. This has now become difficult.

"2.   Previously there were few arguments, conflicts, and disputes among the various households, and those that did arise were easily solved. Now there are many conflicts and they are tough to solve.

"3.   It is more difficult to keep watch over the utilization of land. In the past the land was managed by the workteam and there could be no encroachment. Now one finds peasants using the land to manufacture sun-dried bricks and thereby ruining it. On occasion, families have also built houses on the land they were allotted.

"4.   It is now hard to procure the land needed for essential, collective construction.

"5.   The number of schoolchildren in the rural areas has fallen.

"6.   It is more difficult to carry out birth-control programs. There are fewer opportunities for reward and punishment. In the past the workteam was able to deduct the fines directly from what was to be distributed. Now cadres must go from house to house and request people to pay their fines. This has proven irksome. We have discussed this problem and agreed that what we can do with those who do not pay their fines is to refuse them the right to purchase fertilizer. That should force them to pay up.

"But ideological work remains the most important task of all. We have mentioned administrative measures, but the ideological effort is decisive. Consequently, we now have a full-time cadre in each people's commune who concentrates on the ideological aspects of birth control."

WHERE A DYNASTY
WAS FOUNDED

It was from here, Fengyang District, that the beggar, monk, and warrior originated, the man who united China and became the first emperor of the great Ming dynasty. In 1368 Zhu Yauanzhang, Emperor Tai Zu, founded the dynasty, and in the following year he began the construction of his magnificent capital here. For five years they built Zhongdu: a city with a palace, walls, and strong fortifications, a city that covered thirty square miles. But in 1375 the emperor changed his mind, abandoned his capital, and had a new one built in Nanjing. He had it built to resemble Zhongdu, however, and when the dynasty transferred the capital from Nanjing to Peking in 1421, imperial Peking was modeled on Nanjing, which earlier had been modeled on Zhongdu.

The first capital has now been rediscovered. Archeological excavations have begun. In March 1982 Zhongdu was declared a national historical monument. Zhongdu is much talked of; one hears talk of Emperor Tai Zu, stories about him. We visit his ancestral grave with its path of spirits flanked with stone sculptures. These, the earliest Ming-tomb animal and human figures, are more austere and stylized than those of the Nanjing Ming tombs, which are themselves more interesting than those of the Ming tombs outside Peking.

Yes, it was from here Tai Zu originated. And the city was located here; and the tombs are here; and the sculptures are fascinating, and they were known, although seldom visited by foreigners in recent years, when the entire area was closed.

However, the Ming dynasty was the last great Han Chinese dynasty. It united the old China and reestablished peace. And it was to this dynasty that the patriots and insurgents under the Qing dynasty looked back for inspiration.

It might just be a coincidence that it is this particular district,

Stone sculpture of a general, on the way up to the first Ming emperor's ancestral tomb (ca. 1370). Damiao People's Commune, Fengyang District. The old Ming capital of Zhongdu was only recently declared a national historical monument.

To prevent flooding and make possible irrigation in times of drought, the decision was made in 1970 (during the Cultural Revolution) to carry out the large Hui River Project. In 1973 the construction work began. The river is now under control and 50,000 mu have been reclaimed. The responsible technicians have been working here since the Cultural Revolution.

Wang Zhangtai, vice-chairman of Fengyang District. He is an advocate of the contract system.

The party secretary of Zhangyong workteam, Damiao People's Commune, explains the principles guiding the social services.

Zhang Qihai, forty years old. Upon the healthy, strong, and diligent, the contract system bestows prosperity and, in time, riches.

In the poorest of workteams, Houyang workteam, Xisong Brigade, Damiao People's Commune, the former bookkeeper has now become a rich peasant and has been able to build this two-story, two-family house out in the field.

A young peasant of a new type. He makes his living partly as a hauling contractor, partly as a photographer.

Mao was wrong. I know. Before, I was a cadre; now, I'm rich.

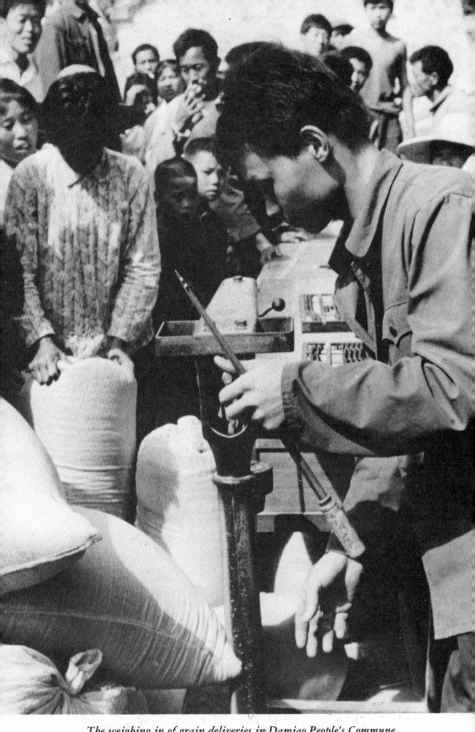

The weighing in of grain deliveries in Damiao People's Commune.

the native place of the first emperor of the great Ming dynasty, that has now been made a national model for the restoration of an effective, well-proven agricultural policy, following a period of confusion and error. It might also be another coincidence that just when the district has been given the role of a political-economic model, the remains of the first Ming emperor's original capital (itself once a model) have been declared a national monument.

But I just can't quite believe in coincidences such as these—especially not in a country as conscious of its past as China.

I make several stops in Fengyang District. I visit people's communes, brigades, and individual peasants who work according to the new contract system. I listen and take notes. But I am unable to form a comprehensive picture; I lack a point of reference. I have never been here before. I am told that only a few years earlier, conditions here were so wretched that the peasants were given official "begging certificates" and went around asking alms. Now I am shown overflowing grain silos and am told that everything has changed. I have no cause to doubt either claim, but I cannot get them to jibe.

I want to make an important point here: my hosts were not lying. One is seldom lied to in China. It has almost never happened to me. One usually receives truthful answers to the question one poses. But it is a problem of posing the right questions, of grasping the decisive issues. Here in Fengyang District, I never succeeded in asking those questions that would have made things clear to me. I still do not understand which factors were responsible for making Fengyang first so miserable and then suddenly so exemplary. I believe that the explanation lies in the local political situation, but that situation is unknown to me. Nor do I know which questions to ask in order to be told the relevant answers. It is not like in Liu Lin, where I have known people a couple of decades and know which policies they followed that particular year, or that, or that.

But although I did not succeed in getting a clear, overall view, or in understanding just exactly how Fengyang was able to make its leap, I was able to gain a number of insights that answered some questions as well as raising new ones.

"In detail, how does the general plan guide the individual contract peasant?"

"We have quite a detailed production plan. He can follow that. But the contract peasant's obligation, in the true sense of the word, is only expressed in terms of quantity of grain or crops. He is free to make his own choices, depending on profitability and competence. We use price as a control mechanism. In the past there was a high demand for soybeans and the price was high. Now our storerooms are filled and we've lowered the price. Thus, the peasants are diverted to other crops. This provides security for the average peasant but also opportunities for really profitable initiatives on the part of those showing enterprise. In this way, some can grow rich quickly and thus serve as models."

Zhang Qihai is forty years old. He is a powerful man, healthy and strong. His household is counted as two-and-a-half able-bodied workers. He has 18 mu, of which 16.8 mu are contracted and 1.2 mu are a private plot. This year he has built himself a house. The house has a tile roof. Now he is planning to buy a sewing machine. When electricity has been brought in, he intends to acquire a television set. He will also buy a tractor.

"Things are better nowadays," he says. "I make my own decisions. I can fertilize at exactly the right moment. No one tells me what to do. Nothing goes to waste; no time is wasted; no one interferes. I know what I have to do in order to reap a good harvest."

The total value of his production in 1981 was 6,000 ¥. This does not include the family food. After deducting various expenses there remained 4,500 ¥ in net income.

The state agricultural tax is 410 jin of grain. He is obliged to sell another 509 jin to the state at a price of 0.12 ¥ per jin. His general production quota is 11,400 jin.

"It would be impossible not to exceed that quota," he says. "For me, at least.'"

Every year he must make the following payments:

14.56 ¥ to the collective fund
8.07 ¥ to the workteam's welfare fund

38.74 ¥ to the fund for payment of various subsidies, including the salaries of the brigade's cadres

7.41 ¥ to the fund for payment of various subsidies within the workteam

He has 5 mu of irrigated land in rice. It requires water twice a year, and each time he must pay 5 ¥ per mu to the team, which then hands on the money.

"Things are going well for us," he says.

"He is far from being the most successful of the peasants," comment the cadres.

"This is a society for the young, healthy, strong, and competent," notes my wife, Gun.

At another place we meet a man who had been a cadre for twenty years but who now has become a contract peasant and is well off. He speaks with intense, muted enthusiasm:

"In the past, there were foremen, bookkeepers, and all kinds of cadres. But now they are no longer needed. Everyone used to be so lazy and no one wanted to work. The leader would blow his whistle, but the peasant would just turn over in his bed and go on snoring. The leader would blow again, and the peasant would step outside and look at the weather. Then the leader blew a third time and the peasant would smoke a pipeful of tobacco. When the leader whistled a few more times, the peasant condescended to plod toward the field, but he moved very slowly and worked as little as possible and then went home as fast as he could. Still, everyone received ten workpoints. The lazy ones earned as much as those who really worked.

"And those who ran around blowing their whistles and reckoning—they too had to be fed. But the peasants had no taste for work. Everyone who could tried to become a cadre and get out of working. Now everyone is forced to be diligent, and one person doesn't make all the decisions. Now each household decides for itself.

"The farming is also done more scientifically."

At this point his enthusiasm for the new policies was so great, and his contempt for the old so pronounced, that I asked:

"In other words, the agricultural policies advocated by Chairman Mao were totally wrong?"

For a moment the room fell silent, and then a district cadre replied:

"Perhaps we have differing views on the question of principle."

"No," I said. "Right now I have no opinion on Chinese agriculture other than desiring to hear what you think. That is why I ask if I should take this to mean that Chairman Mao's policies were totally erroneous."

But I received no answer to this query.

However, a moment later, another former cadre raised the issue again. He had built his house in 1980. The harvests were better now; the seed for sowing better, too. Now one could use night soil as well as fertilizer. In the past, one reluctantly used the precious night soil in the fields, saving it instead for exclusive use on the private plots.

"And now everyone works. In the past, we were up to full strength only at harvest time. Most people stayed home. We have found that we now have more cash and grain, and that we are the first generation to be able to live in proper housing. Our standard of living has improved in recent years.

"If it weren't for socialism, China would not be what she is today. That is certain. But we have lost more than twenty years in agriculture. We followed erroneous policies over this long period of time. They were wrong in two ways.

"Politically, they were wrong in taking class struggle as the decisive link. This was a mistake, since after 1956 China was no longer a society characterized by class struggle. After 1956 the main contradiction in society was that between need and low productivity. Consequently, after 1956 we should have taken productivity as the decisive link in our work and concentrated all our efforts on raising productivity. But this wasn't done.

"The second fundamental error was that policies were carried out using commando methods and through centralization. Everything became a matter of administrative measures, based on central directives. All feeling for initiative was stifled.

"These two errors were corrected in December 1978. Still, we

48

continue along the socialist road, and the foundation remains the collective economy. The land has not been transformed into private property. The fact that we are now paid according to work performed does not mean that the working man receives the entire fruit of his labor. Part of it goes to the state and another part to the collective. This is necessary in order to be able to carry out the large-scale, collective construction projects, for instance.

"The free market is utilized as a supplement. This is also true for the contract peasant. First he must meet his quota, then he can make his own choices. If someone were to concentrate solely on the cultivation of tobacco, which pays well, arguing that he could purchase grain to meet his quota, we would take measures to prevent this. We have to be vigilant, after all."

TRENDS

The trucks stand there in a kilometer-long line. The drivers sleep in the cabs or sit in the road playing cards. The trucks come from various brigades and are delivering tobacco. But it is Sunday and the scale is closed.

On Monday the trucks are still standing there. The drivers sleep in the cabs or play cards in the road. Perhaps something has gone wrong at the factory. It looks like it has shut down.

On Tuesday the trucks are still standing there when we drive by on our way to Damiao (Great Temple) People's Commune. The first Ming emperor had a temple built there for his ancestors. The commune is made up of 9 brigades, 89 workteams, 2,100 households, and 10,772 inhabitants. Production has more than doubled from 1977 to 1981.

"Nineteen seventy-seven was a good year, with a harvest of 9.9 million jin. In 1978 we reaped 8.35 million jin, but in 1979, when we introduced a system of production quotas assigned to the workteams, our harvest increased to 12.65 million jin, and then to 15.35 million jin in 1980. In 1981 we went over to contracting directly with the individual households, and our production climbed to 19.34 million jin. Facts prove that this policy is correct. Per-capita production is now 1,800 jin, with 920 jin per person being delivered to the state. Now, in 1982, we are reckoning on a harvest of at least 22 million jin."

Outside the commune's silo and weighing facilities there snaked a long line of peasants. They had come with grain sacks loaded on wheelbarrows, hand carts, and tractor wagons. They had been waiting all day. Some of them had already been there the day before. All the small roads were jammed with peasants pushing and pulling their carts, while tractors coughed and people shouted at one another. But although this was a record harvest that was being delivered, and the state paid better than the free market, there was no atmosphere of gaiety.

"There is no market for grain here. No one is buying. All the storehouses are filled," said the party secretary. "The peasants are very critical of us now. And they are right. The transportation system does not work; we can't get rid of our stock. Just look at these peanuts. They're last year's crop. They're already spoiling. And the grain is being stored out in the open with only a tarpaulin to protect it. The central planning is at fault. There are no railroad cars. The harvest is rotting. We don't have enough silos, nor enough people to do the weighing. The peasants produce and are paid, but that's as far as it goes.

"We have protested most strongly to the authorities, but nothing happens. Things just keep going badly. And here in the commune there is nothing we can do to solve the problems on our own."

Zhangyong workteam was a poor mud village, part of a poverty-stricken, still-backward people's commune, notorious for its indigence, in a district said to have grown so poor that its inhabitants had been forced to beg and accept emergency help to keep from starving.

"The girl in charge of the workteam's family-planning effort is not from here," said the party secretary. "She is from Shanghai. She fell in love with a local boy, got married, and stayed."

"That's unusual," I commented.

"No," replied the party secretary, "not that unusual. There are about two hundred girls from Shanghai who settled down in this area and got married, and some boys stayed, too. Many of them now hold responsible positions. After all, they are educated."

Later, when we discussed this on the way home, Gun said: "In the Yanan area, no one from the city settled down in any brigade. No one had even heard of such a thing. Why, even Li Lin, who wanted to stay, who fell in love and put down roots, even she left. But in Fengyang, the girls stayed. It seems that Mao Zedong at least succeeded with that integration there. But have you considered what this means? Only the very pick of the young people came to Yanan; it was the children of the upper cadres who went there. The political activists chose to go there. Why, we ourselves know many people who fought to get there, or to have their children sent there, and who failed. It was considered a privilege to come to Yanan, an old base area. But Fengyang was just underdeveloped and poor, so the girls who came to Fengyang were from the lower class. They were not girl cadres, they were working girls. They probably didn't sound so revolutionary and didn't have the same gift of gab as many of those who went to Yanan to learn from the masses, as they called it. The working girls from Shanghai's slums settled down and integrated with the poor peasants, while the children of the cadres only dropped in on the masses. Perhaps that's the way it works. Perhaps Zhou Enlai was also right when he said that one tendency conceals another, and that it is a matter of seeing beyond what is temporary, to the long perspective. Nonetheless, it is remarkable that no one remained in Yanan, while so many settled in lowly Fengyang."

"Particularly now with the new system, it's important that we take care of the families who are having difficulties and who are in need," said the party secretary of Damiao People's Commune. "There is one commune cadre who has this as his full-time duty. He is a vice-chairman of the commune committee. The people we're talking about are the families of those serving in the People's Liberation Army and the needy.

"For the entire district, we have set a yearly minimum allotment of 700 jin of grain per person. The households below this minimum are considered to be in need and must receive assistance. Here in Damiao we have raised this allotment now that our production has increased and have set the minimum at 1,000 jin and 150 ¥. Those with less than this must be given assistance and help by the collective.

"In 1981 we had twenty-five families below the poverty level. The task of helping them is made the personal responsibility of certain cadres at the commune and brigade levels. This year, eight families have been helped to climb out of poverty. All in all, we hope to be able to aid twelve families this year. Our efforts are guided by three principles:

"1.   The problems of the needy family are made the personal responsibility of one particular cadre. Thus there is a personal responsibility to assist the family and to try to help it above the poverty line.

"2. We grant the needy households long-term, interest-free loans from the collective, so that they are given the opportunity to pull themselves out of poverty through their own labor.

"3. If the family lacks a breadwinner, if the man has died, is ill, or is unable to work, we organize the neighbors to help with the plowing, harrowing, and such. We encourage virtuous deeds and show that good people help one another."

Zhao Chonghua of Zhangyong is a single mother with four young children. Her husband became ill in 1976 and died in 1979. She is the only one in the family capable of working. In 1979 she was forced to go out begging. She was obliged to sell so much of the grain she received that she and her children did not have enough to eat. In 1981 the collective drew up a contract with her. With this the family received 8,000 jin of grain and earned a total of 400 ¥ per person. Thus, the household had gotten out of poverty.

"But our task is to get the family up on horseback and then accompany it a bit of the way.

"Two cadres were directly responsible for this family: the party vice-secretary and the workteam leader. The family was exempted from agricultural tax. They received a grant of 145 ¥ without obligation to repay it. The sum was paid out in the form of 700 jin of ammonium sulphate and 600 jin of phosphate. Now the eldest daughter can also take part in the work. The leader of the workteam helped with the plowing, harrowing, harvesting, and threshing. There is no longer any need for economic assistance, but the family must have help with the farmwork for a long time to come in order to remain above the poverty level."

Several cases are presented; account books are shown. We are assured that the new policies, new contract system, and new individual responsibility do not mean that the collective has abandoned the needy or those in difficulty. It is just that now they are free to try alternative solutions. This system of helping needy families up over the poverty line was first developed in Nayang District. It came in response to the difficulties encountered by some families when the new system of individual contracts was introduced.

However, it is the newly rich peasants who are held up as good examples worthy of imitation. In the newspapers one can read the didactic story of the rich peasant Wang Facai from Jiangxi. Although he worked hard, he was always poor. And even though he had five hardworking sons, he was never able to save anything, either before or during the Cultural Revolution. Life was just plain hard. But following the Eleventh Central Committee meeting in December 1978, everything changed. In a short time he had built himself a new house, bought five suites of furniture for his sons, filled twenty cases with new furniture, and had 30,000 ¥ in the bank and cash at home.

But Wang did not become selfish when he got rich. He was just as willing to help others as before. He often made suggestions as to how his neighbors could improve their rice harvests so that they too might become rich. In his free time he worked as a book-keeper for the commune. During the heavy flooding in June 1982, he saved many of his neighbors' lives, placing his own in danger, and instead of trying to save his own property, he led his neighbors to safety.

Later, when his house and property were destroyed, and the neighbors saw rich Wang transformed into a pauper again, they felt sorry for him. He had sacrificed so much for their welfare. But Wang only laughed and said (according to what was reported in the newspapers): "As long as everyone was rescued, my loss means nothing. Thanks to the party's excellent policies, I will certainly get rich again."

An extra ideological point in this story is that Wang Facai's name is pronounced exactly like *fa cai,* which means "become rich." This expression is used exclusively in connection with private property. The dream that has induced so many millions of overseas Chinese to toil fourteen hours a day in Southeast Asia and the United States is this very dream of *fa cai.* The old man who moved the mountains has now become Mr. Wang "Become Rich."

We also visit the newly rich peasants of the impoverished villages in what used to be the poorest of districts. They are building new houses, some of which are even two-storied. They throw out the old beds and buy new, sturdy iron beds, with proper, expensive mattresses. Gun finds the old beds lying on the rubbish heap. They are the typical Asian beds one finds from Southeast Asia to China: a wooden frame on four legs, with a woven bottom that can be tightened. They are easily manufactured, cost little, and are the most functional, back-pleasing beds one can find. They are also well-suited to the climate. She inquires why they were thrown away.

"They're old-fashioned! A poor man's bed."

"But, they are better than the iron beds with mattresses," says Gun.

They laugh as though she had said something amusing or slightly embarrassing. They buy suites of padded furniture.

Eventually it turns out that some of them are not peasants at all any longer. One young man has bought a tractor in partnership with his brother, and now they go around looking for hauling jobs. He is also an expert on the installation of methane systems. The advice he gives the peasants is free; he is paid by the state. But he also has a camera with him, and he photographs the families who seek advice.

"They all order some pictures."

He works together with the photographers in Banpo. He is thinking of going into photography full-time. But he still lives in the village. His house is new and well built.

But even the success stories give rise to doubts. Just who are these newly rich peasants, those who really farm? They are generally party members or former cadres: bookkeepers, workteam leaders. It is he who recently was blowing his whistle, trying to get the peasants to work faster and more efficiently; he has now become a successful independent farmer. He has grown rich and can serve as a good example.

"I can just imagine how the people talk among themselves," says Gun to the district cadres, when we have seen the former bookkeeper's new, two-storied house, which was being built out in the field beyond the old, mud-hutted village.

" 'Yeh, that one! He sure is getting his share.' Isn't that what the peasants are really saying about the former cadres who have now become rich? It's not strange that it is just these people who have become the newly rich peasants. Who else has the drive, the knowledge, the contacts? But isn't that what people are really saying?"

The cadres accompanying us do not answer right away. But after a moment a state cadre says, "Perhaps."

"I can hear them," says Gun. "They talk so that it buzzes inside my head when I see the old village and the new two-storied house."

"How do you explain that things are going so much better now?" I ask the bookkeeper who has become a rich peasant.

"We are following new policies," he answers. "The seed for sowing is better; agriculture is scientifically managed; and, above all, production costs have decreased. Generally speaking, only one third of the labor is needed now, compared with the past."

"Could you explain?"

"Take harvesting, for instance. The field that previously required three men a whole day to harvest is now handled by one man in a single day. He goes to work earlier, goes home later, and works faster. He makes sure that nothing goes to waste, since he himself is responsible. I know this for a fact, since I used to be a leader and had to assign work tasks. It was a pain. It took three or four times the labor to get a thing done. People didn't want to go to work on time. They worked slowly. They wanted to go home and eat. They wanted to return home in the evening. Only a few did a real day's work, but everyone got the same number of workpoints. Now, he who does a real day's work is also well paid for his effort. It's worthwhile to go to the fields early; there are many who go to work two hours earlier than before. And the farming is done scientifically."

In the old mud hut of this newly rich peasant there hung a portrait of Chairman Mao Zedong. That was the only portrait of Mao I saw in Fengyang District.

BIRTH CONTROL ALTERNATIVES

Question: Who will not become rich?

Answer: He who followed the party's call, married late, and has only one or two children. He has a small allotment of land and a shortage of manpower. When he gets old and tired, he will be poor.

Question: Who will become rich?

Answer: He who is healthy, strong, and competent. He who has many healthy, strong, and competent sons. On him fortune will smile.

But today birth control is no longer a request. It is now part of a state plan; it is now a duty.

And this people's commune has met and surpassed its target:

"In 1980 we were a successful unit, regarding birth control. In 1981 we exceeded the plan:

"80 women were to have been sterilized: we sterilized 85.

"80 women were to receive IUDs: we fitted 110 women with IUDs.

"40 women were to be given late abortions: we performed 48 late abortions.

"30 women were to be given early abortions: 35 early abortions were performed.

"This year the plan allows for a maximum of 123 births. We have had 70 births so far and are expecting another 23. Our total figure will thus be 93 instead of 123, which is a good result.

"Twice a year, all women of child-bearing age undergo checkups for pregnancy."

That evening Gun says: "I wonder what the women really say about all this. I'm thinking of those women who during the Cultural Revolution demonstrated and raised hell and said that they wanted their own workpoints and not just to be included in the household's account, those who argued that family planning was not just a question of birth control and population control, but also a matter of women's independence and freedom."

"Perhaps that kind of movement never existed here in Feng-yang," I said.

"It didn't exist in India, either," said Gun, "but the women there began to resist when Sanjay and the various international population-control experts went too far."

"The trouble in India first became really serious when the men were subjected to forced sterilization," I said.

"But what about the families here whose women were sterilized so early that the household did not receive enough land, the families that will be lacking in manpower in the future? What are they saying now, those who had faith in the collective and believed that the promises would be kept?"

A BITTER OLD MAN

He is over eighty-five years old, going on ninety, and says he is soon going to die. Still he continues to struggle against his sickness and has not given up. He is a veteran revolutionary. He is respected and retired; I do not know whether he still has a lot of influence. But he was already active in the 1920s, and in the 1940s he formulated a large part of Mao Zedong's rural policies. As recently as 1982 he was out on a round of inspection. He met with us twice. On each occasion we were allowed an hour of his time. He is vital, quick-witted, and clear-thinking, but toward the end he becomes very tired, and as we are leaving, I see him lean heavily on his secretary. Only with great effort is he able to look like he usually does in the photographs. We have a great deal of respect for him. Now, in 1982, however, he is a very bitter man. He speaks of his bitterness and does not care who happens to be listening.

"So, they told you that one man now does the work of three! That now everything is so great, while before everything was so bad. Phrasemongering . . . always the same wretched phrasemongering! Didn't they tell you how people now enthusiastically get up at three in the morning and run out to the fields with joy in their hearts?

"Sure, it's possible to do three days' work in one day. You can do it provided you labor a double workday, utilizing the early morning hours, the lunch break, and the evening. You can do it by toiling twice as hard, by keeping your children out of school, and by driving them into the fields at four in the morning. That's the way it's done.

"The children do not attend school anymore. The children of the poor peasants do not have time for schooling. Nor can they afford it. If they are allowed to attend school, they first must do a half day's work in the morning before going to school, and then a half day's work in the evening upon returning home. It's no wonder the peasant children are becoming dumb, is it? Why do you think the peasant children are slow-witted and dull in school, why do they sit sleeping when the others are alert and quick to learn? That's the way it is. We wanted to change all that. Education and physical labor were to be integrated. Physical labor is important and helps shape all-around people, not just bookish students. But now we again are faced with a situation where some children are destined for physical labor, others for reading and homework. And which of them do you imagine see themselves running things in the future?

"Profitability is now in the driver's seat, profit will command! But when profit decides everything, it makes for wretched people. It isn't the good people who will lead; it's the slippery, sly, and flattering who prosper. It makes for an evil society.

"Now they are going to do away with what they call the left; the apparatus is to be purged once more. But who's going to be purged and who will remain? Just look at those careerists! Who are they? Yes, they are the phrasemongers from the days of the Cultural Revolution, those who said the right thing at the right moment. The Cultural Revolution was taken over by phrasemongers and the Gang of Four, and now they continue their climb, even though the Gang itself has fallen.

"The statistics are misleading. On my inspection trip I asked, 'Well, how are things going?' And they said: 'Now, with the system of responsibility and the contracts things are finally going well.' But I examined the books, compared them with previous inspections, and I saw no change other than that those who were cunning, enterprising, and sharp-elbowed had now grabbed for themselves a bigger share of the harvest. The harvest itself had not increased. It's all a big bluff!

"We're back where we started. We'll have to begin all over again!

"Today everyone is portraying the years of the Great Leap Forward as a time of catastrophe. They were difficult, with bad harvests and the Russian attempts at sabotaging our economy. But if you're wondering how there happened to be such an upswing in agriculture the following years, you'll find that during those difficult years the whole country built itself small-scale irrigation systems. This was achieved with mass labor, which did divert energy from agriculture; there was a lot of waste and many mistakes were made, but China built herself a network of irrigation systems, which later made it possible for the peasants to increase production and achieve a higher standard of living. See for yourself! Make inquiries! Then you'll learn the answers. But nowadays this is not spoken of officially, because it shows that it is the collective road that is the right way forward.

"No profit-hungry, independent cultivator can accomplish the construction work that is necessary. In many places they can't even agree any longer on how to run a sprinkler system, set up by the collective. In the end this will only lead to a great leap backward.

"Yields have increased because of the use of scientific farming methods. Sure! But what kind of science do you have when independent cultivators allow themselves to be guided strictly by profit? It's like giving a dying man an injection. Did you notice the quantities of fertilizer the independent farmers are now dumping on their fields? There's no control or reflection. The nitrate turns into nitrite. Even now, the subsoil water in some places is being contaminated. The collective is essential if there is to be genuine scientific farming. There must be discussions among the masses as to which methods are good and which are less satisfactory, as to what must be done to assure that our efforts will not just be profitable this year and ten years to come, but that they will continue to be so far into the future.

"Production is increasing. It is increasing because of the construction work done in 1959 and 1960, as well as that done during the campaigns to learn from Dazhai. But what is this income being used for? In the cities people are buying frivolous luxuries. People put up flashy houses. And what about in the countryside, where the new independent cultivators are making more money than they can spend? There they are buying upholstered furniture and useless stuff of all sorts. But the country has not got enough money to build schools, the collective health-care system is being junked, and no new hospitals are being built for the people. Everything is being spent on ostentation. We are witnessing a massive destruction of capital.

"We are headed for a catastrophe, since no one is interested in

Return to a Chinese Village

conserving arable land anymore. The cities just keep expanding, ruining all the good, arable land around them. The same thing is happening in the countryside. Every people's commune wants to become a town; every brigade wants to build brick houses in the fields. And now the independent farmers are building their own brick houses on the fields they have been allotted. But China is a poor country. We suffer a shortage of good farmland. What little we have is now being squandered; it cannot be replaced. And now the collectives, which in the past were able to control the ruin of the land and which worked to prevent erosion, are being disbanded. China's impoverished agriculture will now become even poorer, and it is the very foundation that is being wasted, turned into city streets, and permitted to erode. For the money gained by ruining the soil people are buying easy chairs and gewgaws.

"In the cities it is possible to carry out birth control programs and a one-child system. But what is the result going to be? Just imagine these miniature marvels, who have received the undivided care, attention, and love of their parents and relatives. They'll be the apple of their fathers' eye, and of their mothers', and grandmothers' and grandfathers'. With worse luck, mother being an only child, the baby will be the maternal grandparents' only grandchild, too. Just how do you think that child will turn out? Surely it will become the most unsufferable, impossible, spoiled, and conceited good-for-nothing imaginable. A little lord, used to being waited on. This system will create a totally unfit generation, spoiled and lacking in initiative.

"We had little lords like that back in the 1930s and 1940s. They came out to the base areas wanting to be of service. But they were not fit for work. They were accustomed to being waited on and cared for. They came to make revolution by taking upon themselves the leadership of the masses. Some of them could be retrained, but most were unfit, and we tried to send them home again. But now we are raising a whole generation of this sort of little lord and lady, a generation that is getting the impression that China's people are there for them, to provide for them, while they are taught and cared for. They will be worse than the old mandarins, since they don't even have the mandarins' strict Confucian upbringing.

62

"Birth control efforts have been a total failure in the country-side. Consequently, it has not been possible to get control over population increases. Only people living in the cities can be so naive as to believe that it is possible to reward families with more than one child by seeing to it that the more manpower a family has, the richer it can become, while at the same time introducing a one-child system through administrative measures, penalties, and forced abortions. The peasants won't go along with this. Nor are ideological campaigns enough to get the peasants to cooperate in the birth-control efforts. One must prove that the collective can take responsibility and that it can effectively guarantee its members' security and safety. Today it's just the opposite: they disband the collective and make the household the basic economic unit. They make the solidarity of the family the only security for the old and sick and then try to persuade the families to do away with the one guarantee they have for their security: their children. It just won't work. It will end in a catastrophe if they try to force their measures through with violence.

"You know, don't you, there are already bands of robbers about in the countryside: young peasants who feel that if this is the way things are going to be, they might as well make revolution on their own. They do what young, poor peasants have always done throughout China's history: a few of them get together, become brothers, go out and revolt (as is happening now) by liberating a bank or a commune office where money is kept. This has already begun.

"But there is no cause for despair. China's people are a great people, and China's history is long, and the masses are wise. They have learned much during these more than fifty years. They'll just have to start from the beginning again.

"Besides, this new policy of family farming can only be applied in certain regions of the country. In the northwest, for instance, it is impossible to divide up the land again; the villages there are just too poor. They will be forced to maintain the collective, and so there will always be something left to build on when the time comes."

A THIRD CHINA

It was in the summer of 1976 that I first realized that the cadres no longer wanted China to be compared with India. Instead they spoke of Korea and Japan. They spoke of China's poverty, of patched clothing, shoulder poles, and backwardness.

"Why compare us to India?"

They held that almost thirty years of effort had not been able to lift China out of her underdevelopment and poverty.

What I intended in contrasting development in India with that of China in the postwar period (that is, from Indian independence in 1947 and liberation in China two years later) was a comparison of the situation of the two countries' hundreds of millions of poor peasants. It was this that I deemed relevant. In India the plans had been just as grandiose; what is more, they looked almost identical. To a large extent, both the Indian Community Development and the Chinese people's communes had their roots in the same experiences and same discussions on the evaluation of the wartime Indusco Movement in China. This movement produced the small-scale industrial cooperatives, which were built up through local initiative and which proved themselves capable of supplying China with manufactured goods, in spite of Japanese occupation of the big cities and major industrial centers. Both Jawaharlal Nehru and Mao Zedong had taken a personal interest in this movement, and both felt that the experience gained could be utilized in national reconstruction. But in Nehru's India the plans had remained merely phrases—and a meal ticket for foreign experts and native bureaucrats. In Mao Zedong's China, however, these experiences had an important influence on the shaping of collectivization policies and the Great Leap Forward, as well as on the Cultural Revolution and the "learn from Dazhai" campaigns. And it was this comparison between the poor peasants of India and China that I considered the only relevant one.

For, if one left out the poor peasants and did not take into account the peasant masses in the hinterland nor the slumdwellers, who endure and multiply with fantastic vitality on the periphery of the big cities, if one only compared the universities, the scientific farming methods, the great hydroelectric projects, the new industries, and the ability to adopt and surpass European and American technology, why then it is very likely that the comparison would prove favorable to India. And as for the upper echelons of governmental administration, the education and competence of the higher officials, there too the Indian administration would win hands down. The higher officials in India are at least as incorruptible as their Chinese counterparts. In that sort of comparison, then, India might be seen as a model.

However, this is not what my friends had in mind. They were Chinese cadres and they did not know these things about India. What they meant was that they did not want to be compared with a land of rural poverty, but rather with an advanced Asia. They spoke of Korea and Japan. A few years later they spoke of Korea, Japan, Taiwan, Hong Kong, and Singapore. And when they thought of Korea, it was not certain that it was North Korea they had in mind.

The Americanization that became increasingly evident during the 1970s was not, like in the Soviet Union or Eastern Europe, an attempt to directly imitate American technology and life-style. It was an Americanization reflected through overseas Chinese (and Japanese) spheres of East and Southeast Asia. It was not the pop music from the United States which was recorded and which became the exciting new music for the youth of the cities. No, it was cassettes featuring the stars of Taiwan and Hong Kong.

When the cadres lectured foreign guests, it was no longer from a political platform, as during the Cultural Revolution. Now they did it in a more traditional fashion. They no longer encouraged criticism either: "Learn from the Japanese! Speak politely! Behave in a dignified manner! The Japanese know how to behave, you don't!"

In the beginning of the 1980s reports circulated in the world press as to the consequences of the new economic policies and the new openness. In the south, in the vicinity of Hong Kong, corruption spread, and in many places the new currency introduced for foreign visitors, "tourist money," became a sought-after commodity. With this currency one could purchase imported goods; it could be spent in the friendship stores, where goods that were difficult to obtain and strictly rationed could be found. Since it was considered as proof of having changed foreign currency into Chinese, it could be changed back into U.S. dollars, German marks, Japanese yen, or what have you. There was speculation in the tourist money, as well as trade on the black market, but since the Chinese government neither lost anything nor was injured by these dealings (the speculation was limited to within the country, and it did not affect the standing of the Chinese yuan on the currency markets), the authorities did not take measures against the speculators.

In the special economic zones industries were established that were financed and managed from the United States, Japan, or Hong Kong. Although the workers did receive higher wages, they lacked job security and a say in the management. In addition, they could be fired just like that if their work was not satisfactory or if they did not suit the management. It was the young, competent, self-reliant workers who sought jobs here.

One noticed signs that Mao Zedong's China was in the process of being supplanted by another China. But from where was this new China taking its inspiration? Where was the model? It was certainly not Taiwan. There, a former Japanese province of the Chinese nation had accomplished what could be termed an economic miracle, with American aid. But this had been achieved under conditions equivocal to the Chinese nation, and though the government on Taiwan claimed to be the real China and could point to a certain historical continuity, the regime there was burdened with its past. Its very existence continually gave rise to various attempts by foreign powers to claim that there were two Chinas. Despite the economic progress made by Taiwan, and the fact that its regime still has significant support among certain circles of overseas Chinese, as well as agents and sympathizers within the People's Republic itself, Taiwan could not play the role of model. This feature or that may be borrowed from the island, and a political compromise, permitting the Nationalist leaders to save face, and guaranteeing autonomy and a continued independent economic system within the confines of a unified China is, as in the past, always a possibility. But it was not from Taiwan that the new China that began to develop after Mao took its inspiration.

The influence of Hong Kong's businessmen was evident. Southern China and the coastal cities began to feel Hong Kong's growing influence—with both positive and negative effects. Corruption, comprador behavior, and even narcotics began to gain ground again.

Stories of corrupt cadres became increasingly common. One also began to hear about corrupt officials at Chinese embassies in Europe. Businessmen told of deals where difficult problems were resolved with bribes. It was said that prostitution had reappeared: there were many prostitutes in Canton, but also some in Shanghai, and in Peking foreigners could once again buy themselves a girl for the night. Or so it was said.

But these developments were no model. The higher Chinese officials remained incorruptible. They saw corruption, prostitution, juvenile delinquency—not to mention drug abuse—as evils to be eradicated. When all of China was to be switched over to a new model, a certain degree of social disintegration within a number of sectors had to be reckoned on during a short transitional period. But only for a transitional period. The campaigns for a new socialist ethic were accompanied by police cleanup operations. There was no longer any talk of criticizing Confucius; once again he was a revered teacher.

There is a third model for China, one that is neither corrupt nor burdened with a pre-1949 past.

That model is not the Soviet Union. Relations between China and the Soviet Union may improve, they may even become relatively cordial. Mao Zedong's declaration that the Soviet Union had become a fascistic state and that the Soviet Communist Party had become a fascistic party, serving a small ruling class that arose out of the decay of the dictatorship of the proletariat, that a similar development threatened China, and that the question of who would triumph, the working people or the new bourgeoisie, was not yet decided—all these concepts are now included in Mao Zedong's deviations from correct Mao Zedong Thought. But that does not make the Soviet Union a viable model. The setbacks China suffered during the years the Soviet Union and Soviet development served as a model have not been forgotten. There is no going back to the 1950s. Mao Zedong also succeeded in liberating China from Soviet tutelage, and even if some cadres in discussions in the 1970s looked back on the 1950s with some nostalgia and appeared willing to take their inspiration from Eastern Europe (especially Hungary), by the beginning of the 1980s it was already seen as an expended, negative example. The current model is another, and it is not un-Chinese.

Singapore is in the process of making the leap from what is euphemistically called a developing country into a developed industrial nation. It is not there yet. Too many of its industries are foreign subsidiaries, too many merely assembly plants. But Singapore's leaders are purposefully aiming for their great leap. State revenues are systematically invested to promote developing industries.

"We aren't doing what they did in Eastern Europe. We are not trying to build nineteenth-century industries. We're building the industries of tomorrow."

They speak mockingly of the socialist countries' post-Stalinist industrialization.

"It was a model already antiquated when Stalin adopted it. They were able to use it in Russia in the 1930s. But in the other countries of Eastern Europe it has only succeeded in producing unusually expensive junk: steel mills ready to shut down before they are built; petrochemical industries without stable bases for the supply of raw materials; lots of old muscle without a brain. A dinosaur economy, quite simply!"

The Western European welfare states are held up as a frightful warning. Holland and Sweden have stagnated. They are being strangled in their own bureaucratic welfare systems. All initiative ceases. The newspapers report the Dutch social welfare allowance. Sick benefits lead to absenteeism and low productivity; unemployment benefits lead to laziness. A swelling bureaucracy eats up the labor of the productive minority. Just look at Great Britain, where the trade union movement has shortsightedly hindered innovation and expansion and is transforming that former industrial nation into a museum of industrialism—poverty and underdevelopment.

The United States is still an expansive industrial power with a long technological head start. But there, too, welfarism is corroding society. A growing amount of the country's resources are going to bankroll a parasitic social service sector. Social degeneracy spreads, with drug abuse and disintegration—a society that cannot even see to it that the streets are kept clean or that the mail is delivered on time.

In all these types of society a premium is now being placed on stupidity. The many small dummies stick together and lead each other down into the swamp. The good minds are oppressed and society stagnates in envy and decadence.

Singapore is different. It has been decided that Singapore shall be different and the decision is being carried out. The best minds in Singapore have laid down the guiding principles for a different sort of policy. The vast majority of Singapore's population supports this policy and carries out the decisions, since this increases the general welfare. It pays to work, and the worker earns his pay. The per-capita gross national product is second highest in Asia, after Japan, and productivity is steadily rising. The worker receives his rightful share of the growing prosperity. This fair policy means that skilled labor is rewarded while unskilled labor is penalized. Everyone not only has the right to improve and enrich himself but also the duty. He whose productivity is low must accept the consequences and take his punishment. However, reward and punishment are meted out with fairness. Compared with Singapore's organization, Japan's is capricious, indulgent toward the individual, and slack. Singapore will certainly surpass Japan. It can only go forward and upward—unless there is a war.

During the industrial revolution of its day the little island of Britain, off the coast of Europe, was able to become the leading industrial nation, the richest and mightiest country. And yet its only natural resource was coal. Singapore is a much smaller island. But in today's new technological revolution, it is striving to become our time's leading nation, despite the fact that it does not possess any natural resources at all. Organization, ethics, and efficiency are to take the place of natural assets.

It was the democratic labor movement that created these conditions in Singapore. In cooperation with enlightened British colonialists, the People's Action Party (P.A.P.) defeated the Communists and the Communist-led united front. Taking their inspiration from Histadrut in Israel; the Yugoslavian, Australian, and West German trade union movements, and various political and union leaders from India, Egypt, and Kenya (to name a few) —and with their ideological and organizational assistance—the National Trade Union Movement (N.T.U.M.) was transformed from an antiimperialist struggle organization into a nation-building, all-inclusive trade union movement of a new type.

In the elections of May 30, 1959, P.A.P. won forty-three of the fifty-one seats in the legislative chamber. Lee Kuan Yew became prime minister and decolonialization was carried out. In 1963 independence was achieved within Malaysia and Lee Kuan Yew became the prime minister of Singapore. In 1965 the independent Republic of Singapore was established with Lee Kuan Yew as prime minister. He remains in that post.

The leading political cadres in Singapore have all been schooled in the democratic labor movement and in the anti-Communist trade union work. In some cases (as with the president of the Republic of Singapore, the former trade union leader Devan Nair), they are former Communists or Communist sympathizers who have reconsidered.

There are a great many such former Communists in Singapore. Singapore is a state governed by the rule of law—with one exception: it concerns political opposition. Serious opponents of the regime are kept imprisoned until they change their minds. They are not tortured. They are not murdered. They are just kept locked up until they have a change of heart. When they alter their beliefs, they are let out. They are then honored and given grants. They can have a career. Thus, prison is but a way station on the road to the higher positions in government and society.

This did not bother the democratic socialists of Europe, as

long as Singapore could be seen as a neocolonial experiment. But when Singapore proved itself successful, it was expelled from the international socialist community. In Singapore they joked about this. Israel has not been expelled, and various colonial adventurers in the European socialist parties were still members. There were even quite a number of juicy stories that could be told about certain European socialist leaders who had permitted both imprisonments and torture.

"But we are Asians who have achieved economic success, so now 'the Caucasian socialists' see their fundamental values threatened!"

I was serious, however, when I wrote that the leading cadres have received their training in the labor movement, the antiimperialist struggle, and working-class trade union activity and that they have been schooled in the basics of party organization. (The Israeli Histadrut, too, makes use of the *Iskra* experiences.) Without this background, it would have been impossible for them to carry out their program, and Singapore would now resemble Sri Lanka.

The trade union movement in Singapore grew strong, all-inclusive, and well organized. After that, it was changed from being an instrument for class struggle into being an organization for national construction. First, the union officials were given the same economic and social status as the business leaders. It was to be as profitable to the workers' union leaders as to be their managers. Following this, the union bosses followed a new policy and gave their members a new attitude: the future for the working class lay not in confrontation but in cooperation. The working class should not seek petty short-term improvements but rather great long-term advances. Strikes and sabotaging production harmed the working class. The task of the trade union movement was to control the workers and, by cooperating with the state and management, obtain for the working class its rightful share of the general increase in productivity. The labor movement's task was to assure social stability and guarantee a favorable investment climate.

The task of the government officials was to make sure that the investments were made in the right sectors. The native capitalists were inexperienced and cautious; they had to be spurred into showing more enterprise. The government could take the lead and pav, the way for investment in new fields. At the same time, international investment capital was to be lured into the country. It was also up to the government officials to see to it that the companies understood that it was in their own best interest that the workers received their share of the firms' success.

The government, the union, and the company were three sides of the same entity. The market economy provided the best return. The market weeded out the firms that were not needed or were unprofitable. The government made sure that this took place in a way that accorded with the nation's long-term interests, but placed no unnecessary obstacles in the path of the market's self-regulating forces. The government saw to it that neither unions nor management upset this essential cooperation, through selfish, shortsighted actions.

Singapore suffered a housing shortage. There were large areas of slums. These slum areas were also segregated racially. They were like ghettos and contributed to keeping ethnic animosities alive.

Consequently, large-scale construction of public housing began. More than two thirds of the population has now moved into new housing. The slums are being transformed. Singapore is to become a clean city of planned, multistoried buildings and new green areas. But the building program offers still another advantage: the ethnic ghettos have been done away with. The freedom to choose where one lives leads to clannishness and a general lack of freedom. The population's division into various categories is being systematically broken down and those moving into the new buildings are placed on the various floors, with their communal areas, in such a way that any previously existing group is split up and a new group is formed. At the same time, a regular system of medical checkups has been introduced, while checks are made to make sure that the new arrivals do not take in boarders. Some older women who have lived their whole lives at street level become anxious upon moving onto the twenty-fifth floor, but studies show that the tenants' feeling of security is increasing rapidly.

Because a higher income provides a better standard of housing, the tenants have a good reason to improve their productivity. In

1981 the average income of a family occupying a one-room apartment was 623 Singapore dollars. For the family in a five-room apartment the average was 2,168 Singapore dollars. In the one-room apartments there lived an average of almost four people per room. In the five-room apartments there was less than one person per room. It pays to increase one's productivity! For the unusually successful, or for important specialists who must be kept in Singapore or brought in from abroad, there are also one-family houses with gardens.

Half of the apartments in the public housing corporations are sold to the residents. The buyer gets a good deal: 20 percent down at the time of registration of purchase and the rest in monthly installments. Interest is frozen at 6.25 percent per year. The residents usually use their fund savings for this. Every wage earner belongs to the forced savings scheme, Central Provident Fund, to provide for his old age or early retirement in the event of disability. Savings deducted automatically from the paycheck amount to 37 percent of the salary. The possibility of obtaining a new apartment makes this saving more popular.

The policy of the central wages board contributes to the rapid economic development. Thanks to annual real-wage increases, strikes and disturbances are avoided. At the same time, the wages board makes sure that the gap between skilled and nonskilled labor does not narrow and put a damper on productivity. It must always pay to better one's work and to increase one's productivity. Wage policies contribute to the structural transformation. Labor-intensive work with low increment should systematically be discontinued. Therefore, a special surcharge is levied on low-growth industries for the benefit of the expanding industries, and the low-growth firms are not permitted to keep wages down in order to survive. If they are unable to improve productivity, they should make way for those that can.

At one time, Singapore, too, was influenced by the ideals of the welfare state. Health-care services expanded. This meant that an increasing number of the gifted minds in the population went into medical studies; and since (as they say in Singapore) the number of gifted minds in a given population is a constant, this also meant that an exorbitantly large part of the limited reserve of gifted persons was shifted from productive work over to medical care. Eventually, this leads not only to a lower standard for all, but (as the need for doctors continuously rises) also causes such a strain on the reserve of gifted minds that the proficiency level of the doctors also drops. Health care costs detract from productivity. Therefore, there was a shift from care of the sick to prophylactic care. Instead of paying sick benefits, those who were well were rewarded. This resulted in a rapid improvement in worker attendance. Many of those who really were sick preferred to use their vacations for medical treatment, in order to receive their share of the bonuses paid for high attendance. Health-care personnel could shift their attention to supervising good health. Just as every car requires regular service, each working person requires a regular checkup.

In Singapore the European welfare system with its governmental child allowance would contribute to an undesirable increase in population. Consequently, a negative system was introduced, with the cost of childbirth rising for each successive child. For class C the cost was

 60 S.D. (Singapore dollars) for the first child
100 S.D. for the second child
200 S.D. for the third child
300 S.D. for the fourth child
400 S.D. for the fifth and succeeding children

As for the high-income earners, those with the greatest productivity and the best minds, the system has been arranged so that they will have to pay relatively lower penalties. In order to improve the human raw material and achieve a shift from muscle to mind, from quantity to quality, this system may be further developed. If this does occur, however, it will be done in such a way that no social unrest ensues.

The issue of good minds will determine Singapore's future, as Prime Minister Lee Kuan Yew has pointed out. There is a shortage of top-rate brains. Roughly one in a thousand has a mind capable of contributing to further developing society. But, as Lee Kuan Yew

has observed, some of these good minds have bad characters, pecu-
liarities in their personalities, or little ambition. Thus, society can
only make use of one in three thousand; only he can be used in a
top position.

At present, top thinkers are being exported from the Asian
countries to the English-speaking market. There, the shortage of
good minds possessing a proper work ethic, strict discipline, and a
creative aptitude has forced these countries to overcome their deep-
rooted racism and aversion to people with darker skin color and to
admit highly educated Asians.

Australia changed its policy in March 1966, Canada in October 1967, the United States between 1965 and 1968, and New
Zealand in 1974. Naturally, they do not admit poor Asians, as Lee
Kuan Yew has pointed out. Singapore now also provides top thinkers interested in settling on the island such benefits that many
Asians who had emigrated to the United States, Canada, or Australia are now returning to Asia and settling in Singapore.

"It is not pleasant to be dark-skinned in the Caucasian countries, and one certainly does not want one's daughter to marry a
Caucasian! Singapore is striving to become an Asian home for top
minds."

Since it is important that during a transitional period such as
this, society not be contaminated by the decadence characterizing
the societies of North America and Western Europe—decadence
that made cities such as Bangkok and Manila the meccas of European and American drug addicts, pedophiliacs, and gangsters—the
police are directed to take certain action. Any foreign visitor suspected of decadence is immediately sent home. Men whose hair falls
to their shirt collars are not permitted in the country. Magazines
such as *Playboy* are returned to sender or destroyed. The possession
of fifteen grams of heroin carries an unconditional sentence of death
—a sentence that is unconditionally carried out. The possession of
the slightest amount of hashish brings imprisonment and fines.
Anyone suspected of possessing or having used drugs must submit
to a urine test.

However, it is not just criminality that is combatted. Even
bad behavior must cease. Courtesy campaigns are carried out. The

authorities also make sure that decreed civility is observed. The objectionable habits of making noise in the streets and littering are being fined out of existence: there is a 500-Singapore-dollar fine for throwing a cigarette butt on the street. It is possible to train people to become orderly.

"People already only cross the street at clearly marked crosswalks. They also stop for a red light. Noise has diminished and it is rare that people litter. People are forced to behave properly. There are many policemen, some of whom are in plain clothes. People don't know who is a policeman and who is not. So it's better, and less risky, to be tidy and behave correctly."

However, the penalties are not the main thing. Confucianism has proven to be the best way to achieve an efficiently working society. Experience shows that this is the best way to govern a society. Confucianism is now taught at government expense. Radio and television spread Confucian social teachings.

"Respect for one's parents and the correct relationship between older people and younger, between superior and inferior, is not just generally proper. That which is ethically proper also increases productivity. The reward of the good minds is not their high standard of living; the best minds live in moderation and propriety. The knowledge that one is doing right is the true reward.

"Confucianism respects honest labor. It also upholds the family. Solidarity within the family is not just morally fitting, it also benefits society. Only in societies lacking morality and decency is there a need for welfarism. The filial piety toward the old means that only very rarely is there a need for society's care for the aged. At present, society is also encouraging the existence of three-generation families, composed of parents, children, and grandparents. This by and large solves the problems both of childcare and care for the aged."

Singapore is not just a city-state, an island republic. It is a Chinese republic. All races and peoples are equal in Singapore, and all forms of racism are denounced, but the Han Chinese constitute 76 percent of the population. The majority of them, or their ancestors, originally emigrated from southern China, and their native tongue is the Canton dialect, also spoken in Hong Kong. They are now being systematically regimented. Only the national language, Mandarin Chinese (the Peking dialect, known in Peking as "the people's language" and in Taipeh as "the national language"), is now accepted as Chinese in Singapore. Singapore is national Chinese, not like Hong Kong, which is merely southern Chinese. English is maintained for the sake of world commerce and technology. Malay and Tamil are recognized and respected so that the minorities will have no need to feel wronged. Officially, Malay has the same standing as Mongolian has in the areas of Inner Mongolia where the Han Chinese are in a majority. Singapore is the Third China.

In Singapore one can also see how excellent things would be in Shanghai if there were not 800 million unproductive poor peasants consuming resources and putting a drag on the standard of living.

Now, at the beginning of the 1980s, the Confucian Lee Kuan Yew is as inspiring a figure for many of the cadres of Shanghai and Peking (whether they admit it or not) as Mao Zedong was for China's peasants during the revolution.

And one should bear in mind that of the four small tigers (Korea, Taiwan, Hong Kong, and Singapore) now taking off, outside of China and Japan in East and Southeast Asia, three of the four are Han Chinese. One could say that the tiger cubs in Shanghai-beyond-the-sea have already made their leaps and are now just waiting for the tigress herself.

LOOKING OUT OVER LIU LIN

We have climbed the hill north of Liu Lin in order to take another look at the grave sculptures along Prince Yun Qu's burial path. The temple below was destroyed during the Japanese bombing raids two generations ago, but up here there are still some officials in stone, standing and keeping watch over the grave and valley. Several of the animal statues have toppled over. But nothing has been destroyed since the first time we came up here, twenty years ago.

I have not found out during which ruling period he died, or why he was buried here. He was a young magistrate for Heijian District, in present-day Hubei, during the Ming dynasty. He belonged to the emperor's family. It says so in the epitaph. That is all I know about him. I have repeatedly suggested that the tomb be declared a protected monument. But China has many monuments, and these sculptures are not going bad. Besides, the brigade seems a bit anxious about what may result if the archeologists have it declared a protected monument. People might not be allowed to remain living there. That is what usually happens. That is what happened to the families who used to live at the Ten Thousand Buddha Cave in Yanan. They all had to move and, where they once had lived, there were built new temples and summer houses and it was all declared a protected monument; people were not even allowed to take pictures of it. I have argued that a compromise could be struck by setting up a small sign telling who Prince Yun Qu was and pointing out the way to the burial path and stone sculptures. But Feng Changye looked as mistrustful as Li Youhua had before him. It is as though they did not believe that archeologists knew how to compromise.

Over there, on the far side of the valley, the cement plant belches out its smoke. Heavy vehicles traffic the road. The city is expanding toward what used to be the fields worked by the vegetable team. That is the brigade's best land, and that is where the train is to run. From up here one can see the commune's newly built administration building, so it is not just the city that is spreading out over the fields. Even the buildings of Liu Lin have spilled out into the fields and have begun to spread.

"Do you think the old man was right?" asks Gun.

A group of Swedish tourists that had visited Liu Lin in June 1980 reported that Feng Changye had said that the party's many about-faces were enough to give one a headache. The cadres in the countryside were the sufferers and had to attempt to explain the reversals in policy. It would be better if the party made firm decisions and stuck to its standpoint. At that time, in the summer of 1981, the people of Liu Lin were discussing how to evaluate Mao Zedong. There were two views. One maintained that Mao had been completely correct. The other that Mao had made certain errors and some of them were serious ones.

In 1981 opinion in Liu Lin held that the central agricultural policies created problems, including problems concerning family planning. They were free to choose to institute the new system of responsibility, or not. A third of the people's communes around Yanan had begun with the new system, but it was not being used in Liu Lin. The city dwellers liked the new system, it was said, because it provided them with better vegetables; the peasants could earn more, and the attitude of the government was also positive. But it did not really suit Liu Lin. There, they had enjoyed a 20 to 30 percent annual increase in yields without the new system.

"If we were to disband the workteams in agriculture and go over to family contract farming, it would deal a severe blow to our family planning effort. The new system would mean that every additional able-bodied individual provided the family with extra income," Feng Changye had said on June 8, 1981.

But he had also said: "We must implement party policy."

PARTY SECRETARY LI QISHENG DISCUSSES PRODUCTION RESULTS FOR 1982

Li Qisheng is the son of Li Xingzheng. He grew up in Liu Lin and went to school here. While attending middle school in Yanan, he was a leading red guard, and in 1967 he was sent to Xian's party committee as representative for Yanan's red guards, to help them with the Cultural Revolution and to see to it that their criticism had its proper effect. In 1968 he returned to Liu Lin as a teacher. In 1975 he held the post of assistant party secretary, and in 1978 he was party secretary (having first taken the post in 1977). On September 5, 1982, he described the situation in Liu Lin this way:

"The brigade has six workteams in four villages. That is 220 households with a total population of 1,045. Of these, 530 take part in labor. Since 1979 we have gradually been able to oppose ultraleftist tendencies and to institute a system of responsibility. This has resulted in a significant increase in yields.

"In 1979 we harvested 1.13 million jin [565 tons] of grain.
"In 1980 we harvested 1.18 million jin [590 tons] of grain.
"In 1981 we harvested 945,000 jin [472.5 tons] of grain.

"In 1980 we had rain and bad harvest weather. And yet, the average harvest for these years was 26.7 percent higher than that of 1978." (The harvest in 1978 was 856,400 jin [428.2 tons].)

According to the former plan to increase yields for the years 1975–1980, grain production was to have reached 1.5 million jin (750 tons) by 1980. Of this 550,000 jin (275 tons) was to have been delivered to the state.

On June 11, 1978, Li Qisheng had had this to say about that production goal: "There is a discussion now in progress in the brigade about the plan and our possibilities of fulfilling it. There are two views. There are some who feel that we must be content with reaching 1.3 million jin [650 tons]. Those who feel that we must set our sights on the more modest goal feel that experience up until now shows that the plan is unrealistic. We have not been able to produce more than 1,004,000 jin [502 tons]—and, besides, the weather has been bad. But those who believe that we can fulfill the plan argue that we will have more machines, more acreage, as well as more irrigated fields, in 1980, and that if we work very hard, we can reach our target.

"This is now being discussed at various levels. The party has gone to the people with all the arguments, both for the higher and the lower goals. It is a matter of being able to make the correct decision based on actual conditions. The first step is to bring the question up for discussion. We can make the final decision first when we are able to determine what this year's harvest will be. We will make this decision in October 1."

(That is what Li Qisheng said in 1978. Statistics show that the actual result for 1980 was 70 tons below the revised target, and 170 tons below the higher goal for 1980, and that the result for 1981 was as much below the original plan for 1980 as the amount stipulated by the 1980 plan to be delivered to the state: a total harvest of 472.5 tons instead of 750 tons, of which 275 tons were to have been delivered to the state. If the state planners were counting on this contribution, and if Liu Lin's result was at all typical, then it is easy to understand why the government was forced to make such drastic reductions in 1980 and 1981. Huge projects were canceled or postponed, and the budget for 1981 was cut back by 13.4 percent.)

"Total production value, however, has not shown any great increase over this period. Grain harvests have increased, but our other production has not gone well. There have been serious disruptions. Our workshop, for example, has not been utilized to capacity. Total production value of sidelines was in:

1978: 380,000 ¥
1979: 390,000 ¥
1980: 495,000 ¥
1981: 350,000 ¥"

(On July 1, 1975, Li Qisheng had said: "The plan we have discussed and democratically adopted for the period 1975–1980 establishes that in 1980 we will have a cash income of 500,000 ¥ from sideline production, such as the workshop and the noodle factory.")

"We deliver 145,000 jin (72.5 tons) of grain to the state. 22,000 jin (11 tons) of this represents agricultural tax, while 23,000 jin (11.5 tons) make up our obligatory deliveries. Before the third plenum in December 1978, the price paid by the state for grain sold in excess to the obligatory quantity was 30 percent above the normal price. This was later raised to 50 percent above normal price.

"Our standard of living has improved, however, during this period."

(In 1978 the average allotment of grain was 680 jin, 10 workpoints were worth 1.59 ¥, and the average share of distributed cash came to 170–180 ¥.

Corresponding figures for 1979 were 850 jin of grain, 2.20 ¥, and 230 ¥. By 1980 they were 1,090 jin, 2.70 ¥ [plus a 0.50 ¥ bonus] and 280 ¥. The figures for 1981 were 1,050 jin of grain, 2.70 ¥ [plus a 0.10–0.20 ¥ bonus], and 250 ¥.

Generally speaking, every household has a surplus of grain, as well as money in the bank. Members now own 230 bicycles, 300 watches, and 120 sewing machines (it is difficult to get a supply of good-quality, well-known brands). A growing number of households can now afford to buy new suites of furniture, and per-capita dwelling space has now reached 173 square feet. Half of all the housing has been built since 1979.)

"The situation in the private sector of the economy has greatly improved. The private plots have now increased in area from 0.16 mu per person in 1975 to 0.6 mu today. On the average, 0.2 mu is situated on the flatlands and 0.4 mu on the hillsides. In addition, the peasants are allowed another 0.3 mu on the hillsides if they plant trees on it. This is a way of encouraging the planting of trees on the slopes. If all the trees that have been planted survive, and the work is done in a proper manner, the peasant may be allotted another 0.2 or 0.3 mu. However, this land belongs to the collective. Only the trees are the private property of the peasant. This distribution of the land was carried out according to the 1980 census, and everyone was counted. The greater the number of children, the greater the allotment of land. If one adds up all that is produced for the private market (that is, excluding what is produced for private consumption)—the grain, cooking oil, cotton, pigs, and everything else—the annual per-capita income is between 70 and 80 ¥, maybe as much as 100 ¥."

CAO ZHENGUI
LOOKS BACK

Liu Lin is not one of the most economically advanced brigades in the area. It is just above average. However, in the realm of politics, it is a brigade that has trained several cadres who then went on to higher positions. Liu Deqin, who was such an enthusiastic assistant party secretary in 1969, is now deputy mayor of Yanan. He is responsible for cultural affairs, women's questions, and family planning. And the always cheerful "young writer" from the year 1962, Cao Zhengui, is now party secretary of the Date Orchard People's Commune. This is not just a position of responsibility, it is a post of honor. The Date Orchard served as Chairman Mao Zedong's headquarters for many years. Now, in 1982, Cao Zhengui talks about developments of the last two decades:

"I don't write fiction anymore. There was no more time for that when I became a full-time cadre in 1963. Since then I have done a lot of writing, but of another sort. There's just not enough time. But I sometimes try to find a moment to read. Nowadays I mostly read older literature, but it's not very much.

"As I said, in 1963 I became a full-time cadre and began working in the party committee. I was responsible for propaganda work. In 1970, during the Cultural Revolution, I was named vice-chairman of the commune's revolutionary committee. In 1973 I was transferred to Yaodain People's Commune, to the post of vice-chairman, and two years later I became secretary of the commune's party organization. I was transferred to the Date Orchard People's Commune in 1978. At first I held the position of chairman of the revolutionary committee, and in 1979, I became party secretary. This is not a large commune; it has 8,500 inhabitants. All the people's communes here around the city have fewer than 10,000 members. My task is to aid in party building and to see to it that party directives are implemented. The economic issues are managed in cooperation with the people's commune. I am the party's man and responsible to the party.

"You can see for yourself the developments that have taken place since 1962. But when you compare income, investments, and such, the past with the present, be sure that you do not misinterpret the statistics. As far as I can recall, the statistics you report in your earlier book were correct. Why, I myself helped you collect them. But remember, back then the value of a workday was about 1.70 ¥, and that when you render income in grain plus cash, it will not correspond. You can check this yourself, by comparing it with the value of a workday. At that time, the cash income was the total income expressed in yuan.

"As you know, the political line has shifted dramatically this way and that. Between 1958 and 1960 it swung one way, and this brigade also suffered. The question of the establishment of people's communes had not been thoroughly discussed, and the commune was set up without adequate preparations. Too much of the work force was assigned to tasks other than farming. But in 1961 policy began to swing once again. People were again allowed to have their private plots. Agricultural policies were corrected, and things became better. But one might also say that when you were here in 1962, too much was being distributed to the households in relation to investment needs. When you returned in 1969, the situation was the reverse. At that time, too large a portion of what was produced was being used for investment, whereas too little remained for individual consumption.

"But when we look back and discuss the mistakes we made, when we make comparisons with the present situation, we must always remember that today's progress is always and forever related to what was done in the past. It was then that the foundation was laid. Now we see the results. Actually, this is all quite obvious. It was in 1956 that we first decided to plant fruit trees and in 1959 that we started to plant in earnest, but it took a few years before there was any income.

"Looking back, one can say that there have been five distinct periods:

"1. 1958–1960, when policy was taken to extremes;

"2. 1962–1965, when policies were corrected;

"3. 1966–1975, when the worst extremes were experienced;

"4. 1975–1978, when the policies began to be corrected again; and

"5. following the third plenum in 1978, when the standard of living has risen sharply.

"These shifts created problems for the people. For a while the private plots were in disfavor. In 1961 they were allowed, but people expanded them on the sly. Then, during the campaigns of 1963 and 1964, they were criticized for this, and in 1965, during the socialist reschooling campaign, Old Secretary Li Youhua came under attack. It was claimed that his class standpoint had degenerated. In particular, it was felt that he had been lacking in vigilance toward the class enemy by giving Li Xutang privileges. He had sent him out to do contract labor for the brigade. He considered Li Xutang clever at talking to people and at fixing things. At the same time, Luo Hanghong was also seriously criticized. He was secretary for the youth association but went and married Li Xutang's daughter. This criticism meant that Luo Hanghong could not become a cadre. It decided his future."

(In 1980 Li Xutang and his family regained their civil rights, and the labels *counterrevolutionary* and *landowner* were removed. But Li Hongfu, assistant party secretary and assistant brigade leader since 1968, said in 1982, when he saw Li Xutang's son, Li Damin: "That family has forgotten nothing. Although Li Damin himself never lived in the old society, he has never forgotten that the family lost its land. He behaved quite badly during the Cultural Revolution.")

"The criticism leveled at Li Youhua was rather serious. It was a work group of cadres from the city who came here in October 1964 and initiated that criticism. They were even harder on Feng Changye. They accused him of corruption and embezzlement. He had been admitted to the commune's medical clinic because of an ulcer, but they dragged him out of there to criticize him. However, in May 1965, the masses found that the criticism was unwarranted and that Feng Changye was without guilt. When Old Secretary Li Youhua died of cancer in 1965, Feng Changye was elected to succeed him. That year we had a good harvest and everything seemed fine. Old Secretary Li Youhua had been a very good man. His case was thoroughly investigated in 1980, and he then officially and completely regained his good name.

"In 1966 the Cultural Revolution began. As you know, it was calm here compared with certain other areas. And we experienced no violence. Feng Changye and Li Hongfu were criticized. They were responsible for production at the time. The issue of Liu Lin's counterrevolutionaries was again raised. The party became paralyzed and the mass organization took over leadership. There it was Xue Sijun who was foremost. He was responsible cadre within the Leading Group for the Cultural Revolution in Liu Lin. But the criticism of Feng Changye never became really serious, and when some individuals came out from Yanan to take him back with them to Yanan, 300 peasants gathered, marched into Yanan, and said that enough was enough and took Feng Changye home with them. Only one or two people were seriously criticized. But as I said, there was never any violence here.

"When the revolutionary committee was later established, Feng Changye was made chairman, and later when the party organization became reactivated, he took the post of party secretary.

"Criticism of what was called 'capitalism in the countryside' went on for a long time. It was said that it was impossible to take a single step toward socialism without at the same time criticizing the spontaneous capitalism in the countryside. The private plots again came under fire, and when the peasants sold their eggs at the markets, it was described as a step on the way to capitalism.

"In 1973 people began to say that the brigade should become the lowest level of accountability, that the brigade should be the basic unit. In this way, the workteams would be completely absorbed into the brigade, and, it was claimed, we would take a big step forward toward a collective economy. To be sure, we in the leadership were quite influenced by all this. But we also had quite a lot of confidence in ourselves and were cautious when it came to various innovations. Our standing in the eyes of the masses was fairly high, since the policies we had been following for several years had proven themselves to be effective. But one campaign followed the other. In 1974 it was 'criticize Lin Biao, criticize Confucius' and in 1975 'criticize bourgeois right.'

"However, even when it comes to evaluating these campaigns, one should be careful. For example, when it came to learning from Dazhai, one must distinguish between ideological and practical lessons. It was correct to learn from Dazhai how to level a field and how to combine several small fields into one large one, and such things. These are lessons we still use.

"The reason why development did not proceed more rapidly between 1975 and 1978 was the lack of responsibility. There was no personal responsibility for the work, and that was an impediment.

"With the present system of responsibility, most households are experiencing a swift improvement in living conditions. But it is also true that disparity in various household's income has resulted, and that families with an abundance of manpower are much better off. More money is now being spent; people are buying bicycles and radios. In the Date Orchard People's Commune the peasants have begun buying television sets.

"Dong Yangcheng has ceased working within the collective. He and some others got together, drew out their savings, and bought a used truck. His son, Donghong, drives for them. They are out on various runs. I don't feel that it was very wise. The truck is quite old and I doubt that they can find enough work. No one else here in the vicinity has attempted to set up an independent trucking firm, but several people have bought rototillers and the like.

"As for the youth from the cities who have voluntarily decided to settle in the countryside, our policy has been to let them do as they please. If they want to stay, the party will not hinder them. They talked a lot about how they longed to live like peasants of a new type, in the old base areas around Yanan, but it turned out that they were not being sincere. They found life here too hard for them. It's also true that during the Cultural Revolution, quite a number of the youth from the cities were treated unjustly. There were many, however, who did want to go out to the countryside and who came out prior to the Cultural Revolution. You see, there were tasks here suitable for educated youth; they worked in the laboratories and the day-care centers, for instance.

"But this is a complicated question. There is, to be sure, unemployment in the cities. And in the future, when the standard of living in the rural areas has improved, and when science and technology are developed, then surely the youth of the cities will also want to live in the countryside."

LI QISHENG: ON POLITICAL DEVELOPMENTS FROM 1975 TO 1978

In 1975 Li Qisheng said: "Lin Biao slandered the peasants. He said that we didn't have any food or clothing. He said that our country was suffering from economic stagnation. Now we are in the midst of a 'criticize Lin Biao, criticize Confucius' campaign. We compare the past with the present. We used Ma Haixio as an example: In the old society he was a beggar, now he lives in a cave of the new model; he has enough to eat; his family owns a sewing machine, a radio, and a bicycle. So Lin Biao was mistaken.

"Lin Biao said that the government was rich, but the peasants poor. That's just what the landowners used to say. Lin Biao wanted to turn the clock back. At our meetings we compared what Lin Biao said with what the former landowner here had said. When we began to mechanize our farming, he mocked us. 'You are dirty peasants,' he said. 'You are shouting at heaven. Tractors can't be eaten.' We held a meeting to thoroughly criticize Lin Biao and the landowner. Now Li Xutang behaves better than before, but his thinking is still bad.

"At these meetings we show what Lin Biao, Confucius, and all reactionaries have in common. For instance, the belief that the elite knows best, while the common people are dumb. There is also the notion that men are superior and women inferior. In addition, they maintain that the intellectuals are meant to rule and that the work of the official is of greater worth than other labor. There is also the idea of the middle way. All such notions help revive the past and oppress the people.

"What is the result of this criticism movement? The collective medical service is being strengthened. Youth from the cities come here and prove their worth. We have had one hundred young intellectuals here since 1969, and some of them stay on. They make a great contribution. A couple of them are so good that the peasants have chosen them for leadership positions."

(In 1975, there were discussions about the economic plan for the future, and results obtained, as well as the need for equality in accordance with the campaigns then in progress.

And Li Haicai—who died of hepatitis in 1981—said at an evening meeting:

"There are those who, when they have saved 300 ¥ in the bank and have 500 jin of grain put aside, do not want to continue making revolution but instead want to buy land for themselves. But communism is not just to have three stone caves and a wristwatch. It is an entirely new society.")

In 1978 Li Qisheng said: "If one looks back on the whole period, from 1962 until now, we can see that certain cadres and members have followed an erroneous line. However, it was very difficult for us to see that it was at the center itself, within the Central Committee, that there were spokesmen for a deviationist line, individuals who spread documents to us that, in fact, were wrong. Thus in 1962, for example, certain cadres supported Liu Shaoqi's line. They began to set up business for themselves, charged exorbitant prices, and stole from the collective. Later we did not understand that the Gang of Four actually was a gang of four, nor that they were an antiparty clique that, in fact, stood for a revisionist line. Instead we believed in the documents that came down to us. But after the experience we gained in the struggle against the Gang of Four and their ideas, I am almost sure that we would now have an easier time noticing if mistaken and false instructions were to come down from the party leadership.

"Criticism of certain older cadres has been fomented in this manner on several occasions. Especially Feng Chagye and Li Hongfu have been the targets for this criticism. They were not revolutionary enough, it was claimed. During that campaign, they were called democrats and not revolutionaries. By that it was meant that they had made important contributions prior to 1949, and even later during the setting up of the cooperative, but that they were now incapable of advancing farther. They could not really learn from Dazhai. But the masses did not agree with this criticism. They felt that while these older men had perhaps made some slight errors, they were good cadres who had done a great deal of good. They argued that we really were learning from Dazhai, and that it was wrong to call these veteran cadres bourgeois. The Gang of Four sought to cause splits throughout the country. We in Liu Lin were accused of not taking the cultivation of grain seriously enough, and of being preoccupied with sideline production. We then began a mass discussion about revolution and production. Socialism requires a sound economic foundation. We had to increase production for the sake of revolution. Therefore, within the brigade we praised those workteams and individuals who had done a good job in production, and we rewarded them. These were only symbolic rewards up until 1971, but since then we have always given material bonuses. You might say that the Gang of Four had some influence on us, but that, by and large, we weren't affected.

"There were differing opinions on the issue of distribution policy. Some felt that the ratio we had would result in inequality and growing economic polarization. We divided the grain that was to be allotted in this way: 70 percent according to the size of the household and 30 percent according to the work performed. There were those who felt that this did not sufficiently take into account those in difficulty. In October 1975 we altered our distribution ratio to 80 percent according to family size and 20 percent according to workpoints for work performed.

"But this led to new dissatisfaction and new discussions. Those who worked hard argued that they were being treated unjustly. An eighty-twenty ratio was better in theory, but it didn't work in practice. There were those who said, 'I get just the same whether I work or not.' The level of political consciousness was not high enough for that policy to have been successful. We held many meetings. There was a great deal of discontentment and a lot of arguing back and forth, but finally, in October 1977, we went back to the old system of seventy-thirty. The majority was in favor of this step.

"One of the problems of the Cultural Revolution was that it gave rise to an ultrademocratic attitude. Particularly the youth were influenced. When the foremen criticized them, they replied: 'This criticism and these rules oppress the youth and the peasant masses.' Some of them walked off the job in the middle of the day to go to the movies. When we criticized them for this, they answered: 'You bourgeois democrats run counter to Marxism-Leninism and you underrate the educational value of movies.' The youth, of course, were used to debates and could argue better than the older people. Particularly the older people often became confused. Many of the young people did not bother to conform to conventional meeting rules, either. We criticized this. Things have been going along like this from time to time during this entire period. It is not that the young people are bad, but almost all of them have this attitude to some degree. But it comes and goes. From 1966 to 1969 this attitude was common. The same goes for 1975 and 1976. At the moment things are calmer."

(Feng Changye who sat in on the conversation said: "There were two opposing lines within the party organization. I came to represent one of them. It was said that the bourgeoisie was to be found within the party. I thought I understood this, although I later realized that it was wrong. But I argued that the party had to advance the revolution by increasing production, thereby making socialism possible. So I was attacked and it was claimed that I just talked about production and not about revolution; I just wanted to enrich the state. Those criticizing me were some young people who had been influenced in their thinking by the Gang of Four, but at the time I couldn't properly analyze the issues, and just clung stubbornly to my own views. On occasion the discussions became heated. They said that I was using production to repress the revolution. I replied that grain did not come walking to the brigade by itself. There were acrimonious debates. I was obliged to resort to direct methods. I said: 'I'm the one who's in charge. I'm the one who holds the right to decide. Now, you just do as I say. This discussion is leading nowhere.' I gave orders. I said: 'If we do not complete the work according to the adopted plan, we harm the party and the people. Let us carry out the plan now. When we've done that, we can see who was right. The plan must be followed until 1980.' This was not a good method of discussion, but it was the only one possible at the time.")

THE GREAT PLAN
OF 1975

In 1978 Feng Changye said: "At the Fourth People's Congress the goal was set to modernize China and to mechanize agriculture. In conjunction with this, we held important discussions here in Liu Lin in the spring of 1975 on the subject of our local development up until the year 2000. The long-term goal was that we should develop the brigade so that, even for us, the difference between city and countryside would cease to exist. By the year 2000 there was no longer to be an urban world and a rural world. Our immediate task, however, was to make plans for the period up until 1980.

"We finally set the goal of producing 1.4 million jin (750 tons) of grain in 1980 and of rapidly developing sidelines. Our aim was to expand the workshop into a small industry and to better Liu Lin's prospects fundamentally. At present, a discussion is taking place as to whether the general goal for grain production is attainable, but this does not upset the overall content of the plan.

"In order to succeed with this plan, we must carry out large-scale construction projects. Only a portion of our land is now suited to tractor cultivation. We are also very dependent on the weather. Certain major projects must therefore be carried out by, or in cooperation with, the people's commune district. For instance, the district is now building a large dam that will irrigate 10,000 mu. The district, people's commune, and the various brigades are all involved in this endeavor. We have sent people there from our construction team. There are even youth from the cities taking part. This project calls for the moving of 1,300,000 cubic yards of earth. Irrigation canals must be excavated. In addition, the people's commune has other projects going. In order to accomplish them, the commune began in 1977 to build a cement factory here in the valley. It is needed if the work is to be done properly.

"These projects are being carried out in accordance with the plans drawn up at district and commune levels. Most important for us, however, is the construction work within the brigade. I'm talking now about erosion control and the transformation of the ravines into fields. We did a great deal of work in these areas in 1975, and we are continuing our efforts. This means that it will be possible to mechanize our farming. At present, we can only use farm machinery in the fields down in the big valley. In 1980, we still won't have succeeded in making all the fields suitable for mechanized cultivation. That goal has been set for 1985, and we should be able to attain it. However, it is going to require a very great effort in construction work. It also means that we will gradually stop growing grain on the hillsides. We must use the land as rationally as possible. So we'll have stands of trees up on the high hills and slopes, fruit orchards farther down, and, finally, grain and vegetables on suitable land in the valley. Grain and vegetables will also be grown on the new fields we are preparing in the ravines through erosion control and land leveling.

"To decrease our dependence on the weather, we are increasingly switching over to irrigated cultivation. But we must also conserve water. We reckon on 11,000 gallons of water per mu if we irrigate in the normal fashion. If we use a sprinkler system, we get the same result with only 4,800 gallons of water. So we are going over to the use of sprinklers. Our own workshop is gradually being expanded so as to be able to supply the brigade with sprinkler systems. We use a drop system for the fruit orchards.

"This entire plan is discussed in detail by the masses. We present the plan and then the people talk it over. During these meetings many new ideas come up and many solutions are offered. Some of our suggestions prove to be unsuitable and are altered or rejected. But everyone agrees in principle.

"Fulfilling the plan also means increased security and greater public welfare. Not only will all the families have moved into new housing, we will also have set up a good home for the elderly who are without family, as well as a proper medical clinic, with beds for the sick.

"The greatest obstacle to fulfilling the plan is our shortage of manpower. Great amounts of labor are required. We receive some help with the construction from the youths from the cities who have come here to work for a few years. We have twelve such young people here with us this year.

"We set up the workshop in 1972. It was started to repair our farm machinery and implements. In the future this task will be spread so that each workteam is able to handle its own repairs. At present, our repair shop is developing into a workshop capable of manufacturing simpler machines. To put it another way, it is growing into a small industry."

Li Qisheng said: "We began to invest in tools and machinery even before the workshop was set up in 1972. Total investment over the last decade has amounted to 270,000 ¥. Most of the investment has been made after 1972. For instance, we bought a bulldozer in 1976. We have neither bought on credit nor taken loans. Our method of financing the expansion of the workshop has been to reinvest the surplus from the sidelines, such as the noodle factory. This was a wise course to follow, since we use the machines to improve our farming and increase yields. The workshop is now self-supporting. The truck pays for its own oil and gasoline, as well as for its own repairs. We keep a strict account and see to it that the workshop pays its own way. Then we use the truck, we credit the workshop's account, and the state also pays for the time the truck is hauling for the government.

"The workshop serves agriculture by manufacturing farm implements. It does a variety of jobs, and its total income for 1978 is estimated at 100,000 ¥. Out of this, 10 percent (10,000 ¥) is paid to Liu Lin People's Commune, and 20,000 ¥ goes for fuel costs. The remainder is considered a part of the brigade's economy. All in all, the workshop pays its own way."

Ma Yucai, responsible cadre for the workshop and member of Liu Lin Brigade's revolutionary committee said: "It was Mao Peixin who began it all. When he returned home in 1963, he started repairing hoes, shovels, and the like. The brigade had previously bought machinery and had repairs done at workshops outside the brigade, but it was expensive and time-consuming, and it got in the way of our farmwork. At the same time, Mao Peixin was active in promoting electrification. When accomplished, it spared the women the heaviest chore: working the mill. We installed an electric mill. Then we got threshing machines. We also began using tractors. These innovations led to a change in our thinking. Chairman Mao Zedong has pointed out that our future lies in mechanization and that only when human muscle power is superseded by machines can we hope to develop the country properly—in other words, from carrying poles to wheelbarrows to bulldozers. The poor and middle-income peasants discussed this and felt a strong need to set up a workshop. It could handle the simpler implements such as wheelbarrows. It was about this time that I arrived here. I was a blacksmith and was made a member of the workteam. Later we decided to expand the workshop so as to be able to handle bigger jobs.

"To begin with, we didn't know a whole lot. But the brigade sent members to several factories to learn. The big factories were also very helpful. They used to send out workteams to teach the peasants how to mechanize their farming. They came out here and helped us put things straight. We also studied several books.

"In 1972 we began sending people to take part in longer study courses. We sent five people to study three months at the vocational school in Yanan, to learn to work and repair a lathe. Mao Peixin and four others were sent to Xian to learn welding. That was the year we acquired our first machines: a proper drill, an old lathe, and welding equipment. With these things we were able to service the threshing machine, the mill, and various implements and machinery. In 1972 we also bought our first truck and learned how to make small repairs on it.

"In 1975 we took the next big step. It was then that experienced workers from the factories came and taught us, showed us how to cast and how we could make parts from blueprints. They were painstaking in their efforts. There were twenty-two of us employed in the workshop that year. Now there are twenty-seven.

"We are now able to manufacture and install sprinkler systems, and we can also make harvesting machines on a model from Peking. We can repair machinery and even manufacture spare parts. In 1980 we will not only be able to handle all repairs, large and small, but also have the capability of manufacturing agricultural

Liu Lin village, 1982.

The fields that were terraced and prepared for tractor cultivation during the Cultural Revolution are now being divided up between the groups and transformed into small private plots.

The new main street in Liu Lin village. The People's Commune's administration complex is on the right.

Party Secretary Li Qisheng.

Households are beginning to buy small hand tractors for hauling.

The workshop now manufactures iron beds from the material that was to be used to make sprinkler systems. The market decides.

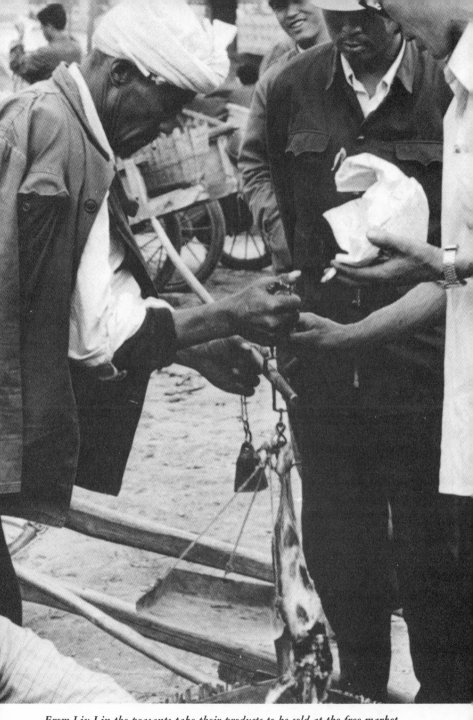

From Liu Lin the peasants take their products to be sold at the free market in Yanan.

Wang Yulan, minban *teacher (paid by the brigade) since* 1978.

Li Hongfu's grandchild during a Chinese lesson in the second grade.

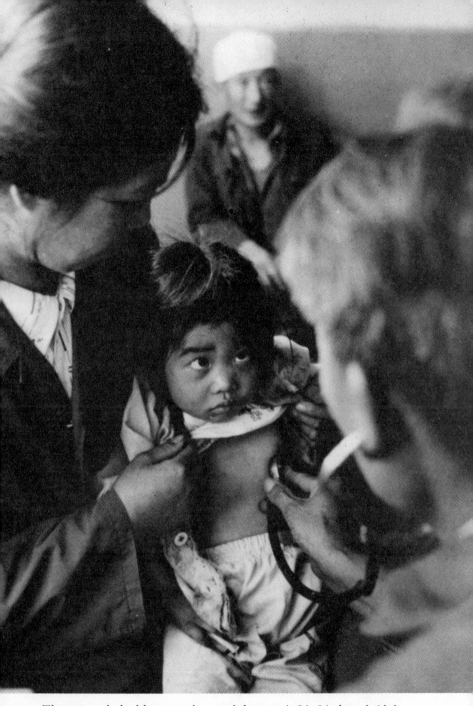

The masses, the health-care workers, and the party in Liu Lin have decided not to discard the collective medical-care system. The health insurance system is maintained.

Luo Hanhong.

Cao Zhengui.

machinery of intermediate size. In 1980 we will be producing sowing machines and plows, and even mills, pumps, and harvesting machines. We are advancing step by step, and, by using the income from the noodle factory, we are able to continue the expansion of the workshop. During the period after 1980, when the brigade is increasingly mechanized, we will set up repair shops in every workteam, while this workshop will become more and more of a small industry. It is now Liu Lin's own young people who are working here, and who have learned their skills locally.

"We now also do work for other brigades within the commune and even do certain jobs for the district."

THE NEW SITUATION

In 1982 Li Qisheng said: "There has been a great deal of confusion among the peasants here. Following the third plenum in December 1978, the party's policies have changed. Toward the end of 1980, the confusion was particularly great; no one knew up from down. Toward the end of 1981, we had a whole month's discussion over which system to choose. As you know, it is in the winter, after the harvest, that people really have the time to talk things out.

"Some of the cadres and peasants had a hard time accepting the system of responsibility. It was especially difficult for them when they learned that in certain localities the contract was being made with the individual households. Some of them then got the mistaken impression that this meant a return to the past, when there was no collective and when each household was responsible only for itself. The party has therefore organized study sessions for the people so that they may understand the party's policies and the decisions made at the third plenum. The purpose of these studies is to convince the people that the new system conforms to the requirements of production and that it does not represent a step backward.

"Even in the brigades where contracts have been made with the individual households, the land remains in the possession of the collective. It isn't so that one is independent. One still must pay the agricultural tax, fulfill compulsory deliveries to the state, and contribute to the collective funds. Nor are the families in these localities allowed to use the land as they wish. They must still conform to the general state plan. The measure taken are merely intended to promote production.

"Our studies are meant to convince the people that even with these new policies, we still have a collective economy and that socialism has not been abandoned.

"Through our studies we are also trying to persuade people that the system in Liu Lin ought to be changed. The collective road was correct, but we made certain mistakes: there were too many orders being given; we didn't adjust to actual conditions, but instead issued commands."

(It should be noted, however, that in Liu Lin this had been a criticism arising from the Cultural Revolution, a criticism of a *disinterest* in the revolution and the needs of the collective. *Now* when the people of Liu Lin are to study in order to be won over to the new agricultural policies, it is due more to a central directive than to a concrete discussion of actual conditions in the brigade. People defended Feng Changye because he had fought for production and not just mouthed slogans. Now they are being called upon to criticize him for his having commanded people to produce.)

"Another error was that we concentrated too much on the cultivation of grain. We also planted too much acreage in millet. This latter is not a grain of high nourishment value."

(The amount of acreage planted in the various grains can certainly be debated, but I never got the impression that the growing of millet had been encouraged for ideological reasons. However, the criticism of too much concentration on grain production strikes me as totally abstract. Just the opposite was characteristic of Liu Lin during 1969, 1975, and 1978: concentrated effort was devoted to sideline production, which was allowed to develop into small-scale industry. The criticism heard then, which was partially encouraged by the party, was that Feng Changye and the other cadres showed too little interest in grain production. Incidently, considering the actual situation, I thought this criticism to be just as abstract as that which is presently voiced.)

"The third plenum put an end to the subjectivism reflected in the line of putting politics first. The third plenum gave the peasants independence and us cadres the possibility to choose various alternatives. We were also urged to free our minds from egalitarian notions. And here in Liu Lin we had been guilty of a great deal of egalitarianism. Distribution was not carried out according to labor performed. This put a damper on enthusiasm. Everyone ate from the same pot, as we say. We led the study of these mistakes for the people, and finally, as 1982 approached, we came to a decision on the issue of which system to adopt. In regard to brigades that had achieved some success, and where the collective economy was relatively strong and the political consciousness fairly high, it was not necessary to contract directly with the individual households. In these brigades, the contract could be made with the various workteams instead. They could be responsible for their own profits and, eventually, also bear their own losses.

"If a workteam shows a profit, each individual in the group receives a share. In 1980 we had a very good harvest. All the workteams received bonuses. We distributed 22,000 ¥.

"Our fruit growing went particularly well in 1981. They had been assigned a goal of 63,000 ¥, but made sales totaling 78,000 ¥. The bonuses there were as much as 190 ¥ per worker. But the workshop, which was not doing so well, could not be given any bonus at all. This year we have introduced penalty fees and deductions for shortfalls. The difference now in income, depending on which workteam one belongs to and what result is achieved is about 280 ¥ per year."

(Notice that the difference in income between the fruit growers and the workshop employees was not a question of work contribution, but a difference in sales results. The market, and not the amount of labor, decided.)

"This new system satisfies the peasants as well as the cadres and gives free rein to individual initiative. But it is still being debated. There is a small minority that thinks that we should go entirely over to household contracts, but we feel that we should maintain the collective and continue along this path. We have not yet completely worked out the system. We have sent out forty-two people, both regular peasants and cadres, to visit advanced brigades resembling our own, places where they have chosen to preserve as much as possible of the collective and to solve the problems without going all the way and distributing the land per contract to the individual households.

"At present, the party organization has its hands full carrying out the partition, for the workteams are now being divided into groups. If one team is split into four groups, how are the grain stores, livestock, and tools to be distributed? This is a difficult task and requires many meetings and a great deal of discussion. It also became evident that more cadres were needed. Each group must keep its own accounts. The party has urged the young people to shoulder this task, and it should see to it that they are properly trained to handle the job.

"There are serious problems with the new system. How are we to arrive at a fair distribution among the various workteams assigned to various activities, such as grain and vegetable cultivation, sidelines, and industrial production? It is also difficult to draw up logical contracts. It should be possible to produce a correct job evaluation, as a basis for rewards and penalties, but we cadres lack the schooling required to achieve this. This is a real problem. The party has urged educated young people to acquire solid, professional knowledge in accounting and to take over this job. Even if one has a long experience in practical work, this job is impossible to do properly unless one has been specially trained.

"A difficulty we are now encountering is that it is necessary to increase the cooperation among the various teams and specialized units. This cooperation is required, for instance, when it rains and an embankment breaks. But when that happens there are some who say that it is no longer their concern. Even some of those who have been with us a long time and who should have a high political consciousness say that it is not their business and that someone else will have to see to the repairs. We must find a way to combine the long-term, collective interests with the short-term profit interest.

"When the floodgates burst, up in the ravine, we immediately contacted the leaders of the two workteams in Liu Lin village, but we couldn't get them to cooperate. It was harvest time. We were unable to solve this problem. We have yet to solve it. They refuse. Cooperation ceased when we went over to the new system, and the burden of the cadres became heavier. As for the threatened catastrophe, we sent in the construction team, and some members contributed voluntary efforts. The brigade paid. But the teams maintained that it was not part of their responsibility.

"Another problem is that it has proven very difficult to overcome egalitarianism. We have overcome the tendency of 'everyone eating out of the same pot,' but are now faced with the situation where people are 'eating out of the same small pots' instead. By this I mean a situation where no individual job evaluation takes place and where every member of the team gets an equal share. And if there's a bonus, everyone gets a share of that. Now we are trying to convince them that the trees should be made an individual responsibility. But, as yet, the party has not succeeded.

"As for the big plan for the new fields and the major land improvement projects, it has been shelved. We haven't done any of that sort of work since 1978. Nor have we proposed any such projects. We are, however, planting trees. Our grain reserve is now down to 180,000 jin (90 tons). We used to keep a reserve of 260,000 jin (130 tons), but this has been reduced in order to allow for more distribution to the peasants.

"Immediate administration costs [that is, the workpoints given the cadres and paid out in reimbursements to those who travel to meetings, the cost of working material, and the like] have not changed much since 1968. The administration costs about 1,000 ¥ per year.

"Feng Changye is now deputy party secretary of Liu Lin People's Commune. He is also a state-employed cadre now. The party has fifty-two members in the brigade, and the youth association thirty-nine. There have been no new members enrolled in three years. In 1981 there were four or five representative meetings for the brigade. The delegates were chosen at brigade meetings. The people's commune draws up the general plan and sets the targets for grain production and for the income from sidelines, as well as fixing the state purchase quotas. The people's commune sometimes also aids needy households. Other times it is the brigade that helps. There's been change there.

"In 1980 Li Xutang regained his civil rights. It was said that he had changed enough. Duan Fuyin also recovered his civil rights.

[He had been KMT squad leader in Liu Lin during the occupation in 1947.]

"Thus we no longer have anyone labeled a counterrevolutionary, or the like, here in the brigade. They have got back their civil rights. This has been done in accordance with central directives issued by the party and government. As for He Talu, who was falsely accused of being a counterrevolutionary in 1969, we reviewed his case, removed this label, and thoroughly reestablished his good name in 1978."

(He Talu had criticized the party and its policies in 1969, and had done it in what was then considered a vulgar and insulting fashion. He was a poor peasant.)

THE BRIGADE'S BOOKKEEPER

Li Hongyi, forty-one years old, has been the brigade's bookkeeper since 1977.

"The six workteams are the basic accounting units. We draw up a contract adapted to actual conditions. The contracts can be made with the workteams, but they can also consist of agreements for a particular job over a limited period of time. In addition, they may fix tasks for certain units. Workteams 1, 2, 4, and 5 were large units, numbering between 170 and 200 members each. Consequently, they were split into two workgroups each at New Year 1982. Workteam 6, which has its land up on the slopes, was divided into six workgroups consisting of four households each. The reason for this disparity is that workteams 1, 2, 4, and 5 had fields better suited to cultivation by farm machinery and therefore they could be maintained as larger units.

"Both the special workgroups and the workteams have their own contracts, and so each unit also has its own bookkeeping. To begin with, we only gave bonuses when the contract was exceeded, but since New Year 1982, the bonuses are counterbalanced by penalties if the contract is not fulfilled. The bonuses and penalties are carefully specified in the contract. They are calculated as a percentage of the surplus or deficit, and they are meant to have an immediate effect on the individual peasants.

"The brigade leadership determines the following:

"1. The leaders appointed to the various groups and teams;
"2. Acreage, distribution of implements, and so on;
"3. Investments (those teams involved solely in farming can receive investments in kind, as well as money, the special groups only in money);
"4. Quotas and tasks; and
"5. Rewards and penalties.

106

"As for the agricultural workteams, the first five have fertile land in the valley as well as on the slopes. They can use farm machinery and have therefore been assigned an annual quota equivalent to 800 jin per mu. If this is exceeded, they receive a bonus of about 10 fen per jin. Thus, if the team produces a surplus of 10,000 jin, it receives 350 ¥ to divide up among its members. If it doesn't reach the stipulated target, we have now introduced a system whereby each member loses workpoints out of a sum equivalent to 10 percent of the deficit. But we must also show flexibility. Suppose a team harvests 790 jin per mu. It wouldn't be fair then to make deductions.

"Our aim is that all the teams having similar conditions within a limited area should reach the same results. If there are differences, then these are due to subjective factors. So our answer is rewards and penalties. If some team were to attain extremely poor results— for example, producing only 300 jin per mu—then it would not be enough to deduct 10 percent of the deficit; we would have to apply stronger medicine.

"But take workteam 6, for instance. Its land is poor. There the target was set at 700 jin per mu and year. Thus they receive less of a return if they exceed their quota and a lesser penalty if they fall short. You see, we do not compare the achievements of workteam 5 and 6. The conditions are different, and the incomes reflect this. Now, if only everyone were engaged in the cultivation of grain, things would not be so complicated. But it is difficult to work out uniform criteria when dealing as we are, with such disparate groups, engaged in a great variety of activities. This places a great responsibility on the cadres.

"We began fixing annual quotas in 1979. We have yet to hit upon a really satisfactory basis of calculation. We set the quotas from year to year, and we are competing with other brigades that set quotas for their workteams. We must now improve our work and work faster, since the competition in society makes objective demands on us.

"When it comes to the construction team and the workshop, it is the government that sets the prices and purchases the products. This year the construction team had reached it annual target by

June, while the workshop is still a long way off. The members of the construction team will receive a large bonus, while the shop workers will be docked.

"The cadres receive their income in workpoints from the workteams to which they belong. From the brigade the workteam receives a sum corresponding to the cadre's contribution to the brigade, calculated according to its valuation of workpoints. The workteam then pays its cadres according to its own valuation of the cadre's workpoints. Since the valuation of the brigade is significantly higher than that of the workteam, the workteam reaps a certain advantage from this.

"Financial administration has become more complicated and now requires more of us. With this work in mind, the People's Agricultural Bank offers courses for bookkeepers. They run three or four days a year. At these classes we learn more. Then I teach those working with economic questions in the workteams and special units. But we still don't have the bookkeeping ability we need for the new system. We only keep account of income and expenditures and some depreciation. We lack the necessary experience. The workteams do not have cadres knowledgeable in these matters. This system of responsibility is very demanding. At present, there are many discussions taking place in which the entire group participates. Everyone should give his opinion of the new organizational forms, and we must allow the majority to decide. But on the question of dividing up the livestock and farming implements, we have had to make some very difficult decisions. Appraisal has not been easy, and it has led to long discussions.

"Since more has been distributed to the peasants, less money has gone into the other funds. The accumulation fund—which is used to purchase machinery as well as for the construction of larger projects, such as the brigade administration building, dams, bridges, and the like—received the following appropriations:

1978: 50,037.42 ¥
1979: 39,955.66 ¥
1980: 20,429.20 ¥
1981: 13,783.68 ¥

"For example, in 1978 and 1979, we built the large meeting hall, which accommodates 430 people. It cost us 50,000 ¥. In September 1981 we had to spend 26,000 ¥ on bridge construction for workteams 1 and 2. This money should have come from the welfare fund, or some other fund, instead. At any rate, it was a borderline case. We now have 15,000 ¥ left in this fund.

"The welfare fund has experienced the same tendency. The following revenues were appropriated to it:

1978: 20,017.07 ¥
1979: 3,669.66 ¥
1980: 3,830.27 ¥
1981: 5,505.50 ¥

"There now remains about 13,000 in this fund.

"The brigade's medical expenditure has dwindled with the new system:

1978: 2,011.62 ¥
1979: 1,128.24 ¥
1980:   26.75 ¥
1982:   15.13 ¥

"Emergency welfare assistance paid directly to the households has risen slightly, however:

1978: 110.00 ¥
1979: 40.00 ¥
1980: 160.00 ¥
1981: 300.00 ¥

"The brigade's expenditure on culture has remained fairly stable:

1978: 3,079.29 ¥
(Figure includes purchase of a television set)
1979:   958.61 ¥

1980: 1,732.24 ¥
1981: 2,437.94 ¥
(Figure includes brigade's payment the year before for the big dance festival in Yanan)

"Immediate product on costs, covering such items as fodder, seed for sowing, and fertilizer, are covered by the workteams.

"In order to understand how we have organized the work, you should study the brigade's plan for 1982. Certain adjustments have been made in the nine months that have passed, but it gives a good general view, and it shows how we plan our work."

(This plan had been drawn up before the start of 1982. It had been preceded by very long discussions. But it wasn't deeply rooted among the peasants. This became apparent in the spring, for example, when in a heated debate the masses [as it was said] forced through a decision to reverse the plan's intentions as to the medical clinic. People thought that it was wrong to run it for the sake of profit. It was decided that it should serve the people as in the past, and that the old cooperative health-care system should be restored.

The plan should primarily be seen as reflecting the view the Central Party and government bodies succeeded in pressuring the local party leadership and cadres into taking.

Large and unavoidable bonuses constitute an integral part of this planning. But they are only for some. The targets are set so low for grain production that it would be almost impossible not to exceed them and be rewarded. The situation is another, however, for the sidelines, such as construction and the workshop. They are entirely dependent on the market. Neither they nor Liu Lin Brigade can sway it. The plan puts a premium on grain production and hinders the development of sidelines. The plan also stands in direct contradiction to the general plan that was adopted in 1975.

This can be explained partially by the fact that Liu Lin Brigade was forced to change its quota system. In 1981 most of the agricultural workteams had not been able to meet their

Table 1. Planning: Lin Lin Brigade, Production Plan for 1982—Agriculture

Product	Grain (in Jin)	Area Twice-Plowed and Leveled (in Mu)	Oil-Yielding Crops (in Jin)	Tree Planting (Area in Mu)	Trees Planted Around Houses, Along Roads and Streams (Absolute Number)	Fruit Trees (Area in Mu)	Calves (Absolute Number)	Kids and Lambs (Absolute Number)	Pasture Land (Area in Mu)	Small Pigs (Absolute Number)	Pigs for Sale (Absolute Number)	Fresh Eggs (Target) (in Jin)	Sheep Slaughtered for Sale (Absolute Number)	Forestation (Area in Mu)
Team 1	180,600	333	3,200	10	1,130	78	2	12	30	37	1	252	7	
Team 2	177,100	324	3,200	10	1,130	78	2	12	30	41	11	279	5	
Team 3	165,300	250	3,000	10	1,130	78	1	10	30	33	10	228	3	
Team 4	201,000	378	3,400	12	1,240	113	2	13	32	44	13	299	5	
Team 5	198,000	869	3,400	12	1,240	113	2	12	32	39	12	265	4	
Team 6	128,000	236	2,800	6	1,130	70	2	10	23	26	7	177	4	
Forest Team														20
Total	1,050,000	2,390	19,000	60	7,000	530	11	69	177	220	54	1,500	28	20

Note: The total sum for grain includes the production of the private plots. The brigade's average yield per mu is 800 jin in the valley and 300 jin on the hillsides.

111

Table 2. Production Targets

Team and Group		Grain Production (in Jin); Special Group (in ¥)	Bonus on Exceeding Target (%)	Penalty upon Deficit (%)	Cash Income (in ¥)	Bonus on Exceeding Target (%)	Remarks
Team 1	Group A	67,200 jin	35	10	2,520	10	The target is taken as a basis for calculating bonuses and penalties. The estimated production total is significantly higher, since it includes both the estimated production in excess of target figures and production from the private plots.
	Group B	67,200 jin	35	10	2,520	10	
Team 2	Group A	66,400 jin	35	10	2,490	10	
	Group B	66,400 jin	35	10	2,490	10	
Team 3		117,600 jin	35	10	4,440	10	
Team 4	Group A	74,800 jin	35	10	2,805	10	
	Group B	74,800 jin	35	10	2,805	10	
Team 5	Group A	76,800 jin	35	10	2,880	10	
	Group B	76,800 jin	35	10	2,880	10	
Team 6		80,500 jin	35	10		10	

Workshop { Operating group	12,000 ¥	35	10	The operating group and the motor pool group share a treasurer and a bookkeeper. Their bonus is divided up through consultation between the two units. The brigade had the right to use the trucks, bulldozer, and tractors 30 days, 150 hours, and 30 days, respectively.
Motor pool group	26,000 ¥	20	5	
Fruit cultivation group	63,000 ¥	15	10	Construct terraced fields covering a total area of 10 mu.
Construction work group	30,000 ¥	20	10	Each worker receives a food compensation of 0.80 ¥ per day for providing himself with a daily ration of 1 jin of corn and 1 jin of millet.
Vegetable cultivation team	8,500 ¥	25	10	
Noodle factory	7,000 ¥	22	10	
Medical clinic	700 ¥	20	10	The clinic is obliged to carry out the health and veterinary measures the higher authorities enjoin.
Forestry group				This group's task is to increase the area planted in trees, and their results are to be inspected and appraised by the party committee and the brigade committee at the end of the year. Area, quality, whether the plan's target has been met, and whether there shall be a bonus or penalty awarded are to be decided by the two committees in consultation.

targets and therefore had not received any bonus. In order to create a more positive attitude in the brigade, targets had been set so that all the workteams would receive a bonus.

But the results attained by the workshop, fruit-growing team, and construction team were dependent on factors beyond the control of the brigade. The general measures that have been taken have the effect of slowing down the diversification and development of side-lines.)

THE FIFTH WORKTEAM

What twenty years ago used to be Liu Lin workteam was eventually divided into the workteams 4 and 5. Zhang Yusheng, twenty-three years old, went through school in Liu Lin and then attended middle school for three years in Yanan. In 1979 he was chosen bookkeeper for the workteam 5.

"I mainly work with farming. But it is also my job to keep the workteam's books. This I do in my free time. Occasionally, however, I devote a full workday or two to bookkeeping. Along with me, there is a treasurer working for the team. His name is Gao Bingyin. He has had a great deal of experience. We do the job for both units.

"In 1981 our total income was 40,502.45 ¥. Expenses came to 9,641.83 ¥. The remainder was apportioned among the working members according to workpoints. That is, except for the 7,000 to 8,000 jin of grain that was given to five families with many mouths but few breadwinners. Generally speaking, 5 percent of gross production goes to the brigade's accumulation fund, and 2 percent of gross production to the brigade's welfare fund. Those who work outside the brigade are still members. If they work in a factory, for instance, the factory remits their entire salary to the workteam, and the workteam then pays them in workpoints. The people working in special groups are paid in the same manner. They may receive a bonus or rewards from their group, but their proper income is paid them by the workteam in the form of workpoints—the workteam, prior to this, having received payment for their workpoints from the special group. The same goes for the cadres employed at brigade level. As for the higher functionaries, they are state employees. But there is a disparity in what a workpoint is worth at the brigade level and what it is worth at the level of the workteam. The fifth workteam has now been split into two groups. The workpoints have a slightly different value in the two, since they are dependent on production. In group A, 10 workpoints are worth 2.55 ¥, whereas in group B, 10 workpoints are worth 2.36 ¥.

"At the brigade level, 10 workpoints are worth 4 ¥. Thus there exists a situation that is somewhat advantageous to the brigade. This money is not counted as income, however.

"The entire workteam is comprised of 103 working members. This number also includes cadres employed at the brigade level, as well as those working in the fruit-cultivation team. Thirty members are counted as full-strength manpower and earn 10 workpoints per workday. These are men. One woman comes up to 7.5 workpoints, whereas the other women receive 6.5 workpoints per day.

"The workteam used to have a bank account. This has now been divided up between the groups. In 1980 the team had borrowed about 15,000 ¥ to purchase a tractor. The loan has been paid back. The interest on the loan came to about 400 ¥. The team still owns the tractor, but the income and expenses have been apportioned among the groups.

"At the time of the partition, group A consisted of twenty-one households and group B of nineteen. Since then, families have split up and people have gotten married. At present, group A is comprised of twenty-five households and group B of twenty one."

Li Qisheng interjected: "On occasion people have wanted to switch from one group to another. In principle, people themselves should not choose or form cliques. This could endanger our unity. We try to dissuade them. Actually, such problems should be put aside until the annual meeting and there be decided by the brigade. But various problems do arise. In the fifth workteam there was the leader of one of the two workgroups who was unable to get along with certain individuals. He wanted to change groups. The brigade agreed to this. Now things are going smoothly, and there are no problems with cooperation."

On the subject of members working outside the brigade, the bookkeeper of the fourth workteam, Cao Ruwa said:

"When it's not high season in the fields, we can contract for other work. In the fourth workteam, we have made an agreement with the city of Yanan to haul gravel. This will bring us an income of 1,000 ¥. We have also agreed to send people out to build and maintain roads. For this, we will receive between 700 and 800 ¥. They pay us according to the official rates for the various jobs, and we pay the members the usual workpoints. We had twelve people out working for two weeks. We selected those who were slightly less than fully able-bodied and who could be spared. We got wind of this contract: some construction work for the central oil-tank fields. We must keep our ears open and try to grab what we can. But the construction workteam is something altogether different. *We* just do odd jobs."

Gao Bingyin is treasurer for the fifth workteam. He was elected treasurer for Liu Lin Agricultural Cooperative in 1955. He has held the same post since then, while the agricultural cooperative became a higher agricultural cooperative, then part of a people's commune, and later when the workteam was divided. And he is still the treasurer now, when the fifth workteam has been split into two groups.

"I'm doing the same job I've always done. That's all I know how to do."

Li Qisheng says: "The masses have a great deal of faith in Gao. He goes not permit any carelessness. He is completely trustworthy, and he feels responsible for even the tiniest grain of the collective's property. He abhors waste."

Gao Bingyin says: "You could say that things are better now. Two groups are an improvement, since this means that the members get a greater sense of responsibility. In the past, when everyone got an equal share, they were not so efficient. The value of the work-points has increased. And now that the two groups have someone to compete with, they do a better job of plowing and apply the fertilizer with more care."

Li Qisheng says: "The fifth workteam was the first to be divided. We did not have to split up the third workteam. It functioned well the way it was. However, it was only the third and fifth workteams that reached their assigned production targets. The first, second and fourth workteams did a poor job of weeding in 1981. They did only two weedings. This year, when they were divided up, they have already weeded three times and, in some cases, four times. The partition also resulted in a greater sense of responsibility in another regard. This has been a dry year. But by the time the brigade leadership decided to take precautionary steps, the fifth workteam's first group had already irrigated twenty days. The members are now paid more for their direct work contribution, and there is a clearer connection between labor and income. This raises work discipline."

Gao Bingyin says: "It's the intensity of work that has increased. People work harder now. In the past, one might see people coming to work just to earn workpoints. They received their points merely for being there. If they tried the same thing today, they would be criticized because now everything depends on the work. People are prepared to work hard in order to get more.

"As for myself, I have a family of four, and we all work. We now get more grain and more cash. I had ten points up until two years ago. It was said that I had become older but was still very competent. Now I earn 9.8 points per day. My son just started working this year, after having left school. He failed to pass the entrance examination for middle school. He has 5.5 points. My daughter, who is a *minban* teacher [*min,* from *renmin,* means "people" and *ban* means "tend"), a teacher appointed and paid by the brigade, has 6 points, and my wife has 5 points. This year there are four of us working. In the past we were three. Our incomes were:

1978: 2,000 jin of grain and 300 ¥ in cash
1979: 3,200 jin of grain and 300 ¥ in cash
1980: 4,200 jin of grain and 700 ¥ in cash
1981: 5,400 jin of grain and 700 ¥ in cash

"I keep enough grain in reserve to last us one or two years. People who have grown up in poverty, like us, always worry about future catastrophes. The old people know how life used to be, but the youth neither know nor care to hear about it.

"I sell vegetables from our private plot, but no grain. This year I have already sold two pigs at the market for 290 ¥. I also buy the meat we eat at the market. This is something new for us. Instead of preserving the meat, we sell it and buy fresh, lean meat.

The Fifth Workteam

We sell the fat meat and buy the lean. We also buy wheat at the market so that we can occasionally eat better food. I believe that this new development, our use of the market, the buying and selling, goes for almost all the households.

"I have bought a bicycle and two watches. The watches are for the children. I don't care about such things. The watches are really ornaments. The young people want to have such trinkets. It's more a question of fashion than of necessity. We do need a sewing machine, but there are no good brands to be had. There are plenty of cheap, poor-quality makes in the shops, but the good, durable brands are in short supply.

"In 1975, when the brigade commenced work on the new village, my old grotto was ruined. It stood in the way. I received 1,400 ￥ in compensation and moved into one of the brigade's dwellings. I have still not decided whether I will build myself a new place or buy one from the brigade, so I haven't touched the money. If I buy a stone grotto with a yard, a privy, and a pigsty from the brigade, I will have to pay a maximum of 1,000 ￥. But perhaps I will build my own. We could use three or four new stone grottos. In any case, I have 1,700 ￥ in the bank."

Laughing, Li Qisheng says:

"If there weren't any brigade leaders here, I bet you'd hear a different figure."

Everyone laughs.

(Bank secrecy is strictly observed. The brigade cannot get hold of the records of bank balances of private citizens. This was discussed in 1975. The peasants are suspected of having much bigger bank accounts than they are willing to admit to the leadership.)

Gao Bingyin says: "Everything is now paid according to work performed. This could create problems for those families not having a breadwinner. But we deal with this problem in another way now. We try to find some lighter occupation for the survivors so that we can award them workpoints. In this way, no one becomes destitute under the new system."

Li Qisheng says: "Under the old system, families with many mouths to feed but few breadwinners were assisted. They received extra rations of grain. Now we are trying to find work for the children and thus provide the family with workpoints instead. If we had adopted the system of individual household contracts, these families would have had a great deal of difficulty. They would not have had enough to eat. Therefore, we feel that our system is superior and more advanced. Families such as these can also raise pigs and earn a cash income from their private plots. Now that we are increasing the acreage of the private plots in the brigade from 100 mu to 600 mu, we must begin to keep account of what the households earn from them. At present, we do not know, but we are beginning to make plans for gathering this information. Without it, the picture we get of the brigade's economy will be totally unrealistic."

Gao Bingyin says: "A problem that has arisen in recent years is that it has become difficult to get rid of the surplus wheat in exchange for cash. There is a scarcity of state silos, and transport is difficult. Last year, after we had delivered our quota—and our supplementary quota, too—we wanted to sell even more. But we weren't allowed. We succeeded, however, in locating another brigade whose supplementary quota had not been filled, and so we could sell our grain in their name. But corn, for example, should not be stored more than two years.

"In September 1981 the government enjoined all people's communes to build silos. In the past, we sold our grain to the district. Now it was to be sold to the people's commune. Our own three grain storehouses in the brigade were built according to existing specifications. They are properly ventilated and no rats can get in. We can store 260,000 jin there for the brigade."

(But since the brigade has sold a portion of its reserves in order to have more to distribute to its members, there remains only 180,000 jin in reserve. In the past, the storehouses were full.)

The Fifth Workteam

"We have made an investigation that showed that more than half of the households have a grain reserve sufficient to cover their private needs for two years. I, for example, have 8,000 jin. 3,500 jin is enough to cover my family's needs for one year. We feel that the private households take good care of their grain. It does not spoil, especially not now, when the cool weather is here."

Table 3. Workteam 5: Financial Report for 1981

Assets, Jan. 1, 1981 (prior to the partition of the workteam)	
Large livestock (oxen, donkeys), 27	10,350.00¥
Smaller livestock (goats, sheep), 108	2,120.00¥
16 stone grottoes	12,800.00
Agricultural machinery, 24 pieces	7,453.75
Agricultural implements, 185 pieces	429.00
Bank account	2,499.02
Grain reserve, 11,396 jin	1,392.83
Debts, Jan. 1, 1981	
Bank loan	9,300.00¥
Assets to be divided, Jan. 1, 1982	51,232.31¥
Group A	25,616.11
Group B	25,616.11
Group A	
Large livestock, 12	3,591.00¥
Smaller livestock, 46	902.00
8 stone grottoes	6,400.00
Agricultural machinery, 13 pieces	12,770.12
Agricultural implements, 93 pieces	215.00
Bank account	1,041.58
Grain reserve, 5,698 jin	696.42
Group B	
Large livestock, 11	3,430.00¥
Smaller livestock, 45	882.00
8 stone grottoes	6,400.00
Agricultural machinery, 13 pieces	12,952.11

Agricultural implements, 92 pieces	214.00
Bank account	1,041.58
Grain reserve, 5,698 jin	696.42

Debts Jan. 1, 1982	None
Production costs for 1981 out of	
1980's production	3,615.24¥
Production costs for 1982 out of	
1981's production	2,869.19

Workteam 5, Group A: Financial Report for 1981

Agricultural income	
Total grain production, 111,202 jin	11,317.92¥
Corn, 48 mu, 46,475 jin	4,275.70
Wheat, 44 mu, 12,553 jin	1,694.66
Millet, 52 mu, 23,217 jin	2,182.40
Glutinous millet, 25 mu, 8,369 jin	795.06
Buckwheat, 6 mu, 653 jin	71.83
Kaoliang (sorghum), 8 mu, 5,132 jin	394.90
Other, 33 mu, 14,803 jin	1,903.37

Harvest disbursements	
Agricultural tax, 1,738 jin	275.63¥
State purchase, 3,420 jin	393.45
Fodder, 5,862 jin	622.13
Seed for sowing, 4,853 jin	560.81
Grain reserve, 541 jin	61.52
To the members, 14,803 jin	9,404.38

Animal production	549.82¥
Wool	376.82
Mutton	110.30
Sheepskins	62.70

Sidelines	5,154.32¥
Income from the tractor	2,774.05
Work outside the brigade for district and state	2,380.27
Other income	2,641.97

The Fifth Workteam

Total Income, 1981	19,664.03¥

Expenses for Group A	
Interest on bank loan	207.00¥
Costs for agriculture	896.53
Seed for sowing	1,045.32
Fertilizer	586.74
Pesticides	30.00
Water and electricity	71.75
Costs for stock raising	297.43
Fodder	281.93
Costs for sidelines	1,387.76
Fuel for tractor	639.05
Spare parts for the tractor	497.87
Road tax	188.00
Tax	62.84
Incidental expenses	42.71
Office material, etc., for the bookkeeper and leaders	26.11
Grants to cadres for conference attendance	16.60

Total Expenses, 1981	4,847.17¥

Remaining for distribution fund for Group A	14,816.86¥
Deductions:	
Agricultural tax	275.63
Appropriation to brigade's accumulation fund	1,652.11
Appropriation to brigade's welfare fund	393.28
Appropriation to brigade's distribution fund	1,646.50
Remaining to apportion	
Payment from brigade for members employed as cadres or who worked in special groups (i.e., the fruit cultivation team) at a rate of 4 ¥ per 10 workpoints	10,914.40¥

Total to be apportioned according to workpoints	21,763.74¥
Total workpoints in Group A, 1981	85,348.00
10 workpoints are worth	2.55

(Observe that the labor of the brigade cadres and the members of the special groups, as well as work done outside the brigade, are counted in the group's workpoint valuation and that the apportionment is done accordingly.)

DISTINCTIONS

The construction team has already fulfilled its quota for the year. It makes a big profit.

Ta Zhenyan says: "I became leader for the construction team in 1973. Except for 1981, when the team was temporarily disbanded, I have held the same post the whole time.

"In 1979, the team consisted of forty-three working members. At that time, we built the premises for the workshop group. We also signed a contract to construct six large tunnel-vaulted houses for the credit bank, to be used as their branch office in Liu Lin. That contract was worth 12,000 ¥. We supplied timber for 300 ¥, sand for 400 ¥, and lime for 600 ¥. It was a difficult job; the building site was half bedrock, half loose sand. We had to break stone as well as lay a proper foundation. It took about 2,000 man-days and earned the brigade about 5 ¥ per workday. It was not a profitable deal.

"That same year, we worked on the construction of the large meeting hall, as well as a number of buildings for the brigade. At that time the brigade paid workteams at a rate of 5.30 ¥ for 10 workpoints. I belong to the first workteam. There, 10 workpoints were then worth 2.05 ¥. That year, the first workteam held to a distribution principle that first apportioned 80 percent according to the number of household members, and then paid the remaining 20 percent according to the number of workpoints.

"In 1980, we built two very large fruit storehouses for Yanan's fruit company. They were each 60 meters long, 4 meters wide, and 5 meters high and were built underground up by the terraced fruit fields. They were situated underground in order to maintain a constant temperature. The work took 2,000 man-days and the brigade was paid 60,000 ¥. But this was a lump sum, for everything—the labor, stone, land, and destroyed trees. At that time we still maintained the same principle for distribution.

"In spring 1981, we built three tunnel-vaulted houses, up near the fruit orchards, for the brigade. Then we tried to find some other work, but there were no contracts to be had. There was no work, so we disbanded the construction team, and each of us rejoined his old workteam. I and the others went back to being regular peasants. That year there was a great deal of discussion. In the autumn, the distribution principle was changed. From then on, only workpoints were to be considered. Nothing was to be paid out, except for workpoints.

"The construction team was reestablished this year. I was again made leader, and we were assigned a specific target: We were to earn 30,000 ¥. Our team now consists of thirty-two members. If we succeed in exceeding our target, the brigade gets 80 percent of the surplus, and we get 20 percent to divide up among ourselves. If we fail to make 30,000 ¥, we will be penalized. But by July of this year, we had already met the year's goal. Everything we do now is just gravy.

"In the spring, we signed a contract with the municipality of Yanan. They were going to build a multistory building down here by the river. We did the reinforcement work and the embankment of the river. This job paid 20,000 ¥. We also built an embankment for the brigade. It was entered into the books at the standard government rate and paid 8,000 ¥. We did some work up in the ravines for 3,000 ¥. With that, we had put in 5,000 man-days and taken in 31,000 ¥.

"We have now signed a contract with the oil-tank unit. We are going to build walls. We are in the process of signing contracts with several units in the vicinity. We have a good reputation because we work well and know our job. One recommends us to another. We also have people out looking for contracts. It is hard to say by what margin we will exceed our target this year. Perhaps we will double it."

Our talk on the subject of the workshop takes place in a charged atmosphere. The contradictions are manifest. Mao Peixin is taciturn. He neither smiles nor even bothers to look at Li Qisheng. He says what he thinks necessary and then ceases to take part in the conversation. But away from this meeting, at home with his family, he is his usual self—glad, laughing, and proud. During the discussion of the workshop, he just says:

"I have left the brigade. We just live here. My son works in the brigade, but I am a truck driver for the people's commune now. I drive a truck and transport fertilizer, machinery, and other things to the brigades. Once a week I drive down to Xian to pick up goods. This is actually an interesting job. I am now also employed by the government, at a monthly salary of 51 ¥. I am an official of the fourth rank, with job security, paid health care, and other benefits. It was in 1978 that I left the brigade. I am capable of repairing my own truck.

"We have mechanized here as much as possible. Since 1962, major changes have taken place. Now our main problems are transport and irrigation."

Ma Yucai is still responsible for the workshop. He says: "We are the same number as before—25 people. Some have left us and been replaced by others. We have traded in one truck, and got a bigger and better one. We have also acquired another 50-horse-power tractor.

"The workshop has been getting no orders. We try to find various solutions. We make furniture. There are, as you know, many households buying sets of furniture now. We have also got a contract to manufacture iron beds for a school. We are using the pipes that previously went to make the sprinkler systems for the beds. We are also trying to find other things to do. We burn lime and haul gravel for the city. They're doing a lot of construction there, you see.

"What has happened is that we are getting fewer orders. In the past we worked as a subcontractor, manufacturing parts for agricultural machinery and the like. We worked for our own brigade, as well as for others, with sprinkler systems and other things. Then came the new economic policies. The small industries we worked for were less profitable and had fewer orders, and so we, too, had fewer orders.

"Things have become more difficult, especially since the end of 1980. That year we had total earnings of 42,000 ¥. In 1981 we were down to 28,000 ¥, but there was still no system of penalties. This year the members of the workshop team will be penalized if they do not take in enough earnings. But what is to account for us not showing sufficient earnings? Well,

"1. The whole country's economy is in the process of re-adjustment. This affects our own work.
"2. The system of responsibility is being introduced in various places. This makes for greater efficiency and tougher competition.
"3. Other units are more cautious now, make better use of their own resources, and approach us with fewer orders.

"We intend to make a careful analysis of the situation. For if the decrease in earnings and drop in orders is not due to faulty planning, ineffective leadership, or poor workmanship, then it is not a question of such subjective factors as would justify the imposition of penalties."

Here Li Qisheng breaks in and says: "Last year we had no rules. Naturally, we must investigate why the workshop has failed to meet its target. But it is a matter of both subjective and objective factors. As yet, nothing has been said of the subjective factors. The work done is of poor quality and the management is bad. All customers now demand high quality. Nor has the workshop's target been set at random. It is based on previous experience and careful study. But, as I said, if a new exhaustive study were to show that it was only objective factors causing the poor earnings, naturally there would be no penalties.

"The brigade leadership has had this matter up for discussion on several occasions. In 1979 we had a major dispute with the workshop. It wasn't possible then for them to blame the decline on a shortage of orders. At that time, we came to the conclusion that the workshop was mismanaged. Quality was low, the work poorly led. The organization was bad. After being thus criticized, the workshop took a turn for the better, which lasted through 1980. Actually, it was the only unit to do poorly in 1979.

"In 1981, it was back to its old ways. It is incorrect to say that it is only a matter of a shortage of orders. The management is also incompetent, and the work badly done. However, in 1981 they were not the only unit to make a bad job of it. Four workteams showed poor results. This was because of conflicting opinions as to how things should be done."

Ma Yucai says: "We do not intend to close the workshop or cut the number of workers there. We can get new orders. We are going to make deals for the subcontracting of machine parts. Naturally, the issues of competent management, labor quality, and machines are important, but until something better comes along, it's better we burn lime than do nothing at all."

Li Qisheng says: "Actually, we need to solve the problem of the mechanization of weeding and the total mechanization of harvesting. We also hope to be able to mechanize the corn harvest but don't expect that we can achieve the same for the millet. What we need most of all right now is means of transportation up on the hillsides."

GIVE US
REAL HEROES!

Qiao Fengcong was made responsible for the fruit orchard in 1972. The following year he became deputy party secretary and assistant brigade leader. In 1981 he took over responsibility for cultural and welfare affairs for the brigade. The man who was previously in charge, Xue Sijun, had died.

"In the past, people were often switched about from one job to another. One year they worked with the fruit trees, the next with something else. I considered this to be a mistake. When I was elected leader in 1972, I felt that the team should remain stable. Since then, we have had the same administration, the same technical leadership, and the same personnel. Occasionally, some change is made, but this is only natural in a working unit over a year period. Still, it happens only rarely.

"In the past, there was not enough fertilization, and the irrigation was not even done scientifically. That is why the trees grew badly. Over the last ten years, we have done a better job of fertilization, both with compost and chemical fertilizer. We have also learned how to irrigate properly. We have been able to achieve these things because we have not altered the team. As a stable unit, we gain experience and improve our work year by year. The number of members has remained the same; we are still forty-two.

"We have no plans to increase the acreage of the orchard. However, we do replace the older trees. We are switching over to better, more prolific varieties of trees. We increase production by improving quality.

"The members of this team have been selected from various workteams. The brigade pays those teams workpoints for their members, who in turn receive from the teams their share of what is distributed according to their workpoints. But they only work with the orchards. In the winter they compost, prune, or do other such tasks. Work in the orchards is no seasonal occupation; it is a steady, year-round endeavor. The members also now receive a bonus for their labor in the orchards. It is given as a lump sum to the fruit cultivation team. In 1980 the bonus amounted to 0.50 ¥ per workday.

"The system is slightly different this year, but we have decided to keep this form of responsibility for another two years. The income from the fruit cultivation belongs to the entire brigade. If there is a bonus or penalty awarded for exceeding or failing to meet the target, it is shared by the members of this special unit, but they will go on receiving their ordinary incomes from the workteams to which they belong.

"Prior to the third plenum in 1978, our highest income was 60,000 ¥. Sometimes it was 40,000 ¥. Since then it has increased. In 1979 it was 80,000 ¥, in 1980 it was 63,000 ¥, and in 1981, 65,000 ¥. The target set for 1982 is 63,000 ¥, with the same goal for 1983.

"Not long after I took over responsibility for the orchard, I was elected deputy party secretary. Since then, I have worked with the same job. The leading group here in Liu Lin is stable and harmonious, and it's been like that for a long time. We have not had to make any major changes.

"In 1981 I took charge of cultural affairs. In the past the brigade administered the school. The brigade was responsible for questions concerning the school and supervised the teaching, although it followed the general curriculum. In 1980 the government took over responsibility for the school, and it is now administered by state cadres. But there are two *minban* teachers left. They are paid by the brigade with workpoints from their respective workteams."

(In other localities, these teachers from the workteams and brigades were being eliminated. From now on there were only to be state teachers.)

"But the brigade must still pay for the upkeep and repairs of the school buildings, furnishings, and the like. From now July 18,

1981, when I took charge of cultural affairs, until now, fourteen months later, the brigade has had to pay more than 3,000 ¥ for this type of expense.

"We have purchased television sets, so that people will be able to keep up with what is happening. We now have seven sets in the brigade. One of these is privately owned. It's Li Piyun who owns his own television set. Television has now got a mass audience out in the countryside.

"Nonetheless, film is still the most important medium. We bought a good projector in 1972. During the busy season, when we have a lot of farm work to do, we have two shows a week in the brigade. During the rest of the year, we have five, or sometimes six, shows a week. These shows are given in various places, so that everyone has a chance to see the movies. We have two trained projectionists. One is permanently employed and the other is a spare who can step in when needed. They have both taken courses in Yanan, and both belong to the fourth workteam. The regular projectionist can be considered a brigade cadre. The brigade pays the workteam points for the projectionists' labor, and the workteam credits them in the usual way with these points toward distribution.

"We select the films we show ourselves, from the film distribution center in Yanan. We pay 1.50 ¥ in rent for each showing, and including transportation costs, electricity and maintenance of the projector, the films cost us about 800 ¥ per year. Sometimes in Yanan they want us to show some particular film, but we generally choose ourselves.

"Now it happens that the brigade members have a very definite taste in films. Many of the new films being shown in the cities are not to the people's liking here. People don't want to see those romantic movies. They prefer war films, and other films where there are real heroes and where the bad guys are easy to spot. They also want to see films about the countryside. We show documentaries on agriculture and agricultural issues, too.

"We generally get Chinese films, but Korean productions are also very popular. In addition, we have shown films on war and industry from Yugoslavia and Rumania.

"It is not so easy to get hold of the war films the people want.

There is a long line for them, and the distribution center sends them out in proper order. They are the ones in greatest demand. Romantic films in the new style are always available, but people aren't interested.

"The brigade doesn't have an orchestra or a theater group, but the youth association does these kinds of things. Some of the young people are good at singing and playing instruments. Mao Peixin's eldest son is actually a very good singer. The youth association works with putting on local operas based on traditional melodies. During the spring festival, major productions are now put on in Yanan. There are numerous lanterns and long serpentine files of *yangge* dancers. The brigade helps finance these events, and everyone goes."

THE SCHOOL

Yin Gaoan graduated from the teachers college in Yanan in 1960. He is now a teacher and the party secretary for Liu Lin School. This is a five-grade school.

"Ninety-eight percent of the school-age children attend school. Two boys stay home to care for younger brothers and sisters. Two eight-year-olds are behind in their development and have not yet started. Two children were allowed to leave school in the fourth grade because they were mentally retarded. Of the thirty-nine pupils who graduated from the fifth grade in 1982, thirty-five were able to go on to middle school. The four who did not pass the entrance examinations were all having a hard time in school, but their parents wanted them to go on studying. In the past, everyone went on with their studies, but now there are examinations that weed out those who cannot continue.

"All the children now want to go on studying. The parents feel the same way. But it's intelligence that decides. Deficient intellect sets limits. Intelligence must be the determining factor in the admission policies of institutions of higher learning.

"The children used to be duller; now they are more gifted. But there is a great difference between children in the cities and those from the countryside. In the rural areas the children lag further behind. It isn't just that there are nursery schools in the cities and that the city schools are better, the parents are also able to help their children more. Here in the countryside, the parents can barely help their children through the first-grade material, while in the cities, they can give them a hand even at the middle-school level.

"The teacher's status has improved. Since the third plenum, more emphasis has been placed on the needs of the intellectuals. Teaching methods have also improved and the work is better planned."

(Curriculum and teaching methods appear to be about the same as in 1962. The present principal is the same person who held the job in 1954–1958. Instruction about the world outside China is nonexistent. Physical education and sports have possibly been curtailed. Pupils in classes 1, 2, and 3 pay a tuition fee of 2 ¥ per term, and fourth and fifth graders pay 2.50 ¥. In addition, each pupil pays 1 ¥ each winter for the heating of the school. Pencils, pencil sharpeners, erasers, and rulers cost each student between 1 and 2 ¥. Paper and notebooks cost about .50 ¥ per term. Books and teaching materials cost another 1 ¥ per term for the lower grades, and 2.04 ¥ for the fifth graders.

The two *minban* teachers hoped to be admitted to the teachers college and so become properly credentialed. The school no longer suffered any discipline problems. Teaching was done along traditional lines. For instance, the pupils read aloud in unison.)

THE COUNTRY DOCTOR WANG YOUNENG

Wang Youneng has grown older; his hair has begun to turn gray. He speaks with great calm. He is highly respected and well liked. And when he talks on the subject of health care, he does so with a great deal of self-assurance:

"In 1969, we established the medical clinic here. Up until 1982 the members paid 1.50 ¥ a year and an additional 0.05 ¥ registration fee per visit. Aside from these fees, all health care was without charge. We discussed abolishing even these fees. Then the system of responsibility was introduced, and the clinic was supposed to make a profit. Each treatment was to pay for itself and, what's more, return a profit.

"In spring 1982 this innovation was much debated by the masses and the health-care workers. The new system didn't work at all; it was a bad system. The party and the masses were in total agreement on this. We had tried the new system, and experience had proven it to be a mistake. The old methods were superior. It was decided that, beginning in 1983, Liu Lin Brigade would go back to the system of cooperative medical care.

"The advantages of cooperative medicine are very great. The primary task of all medical care must be to prevent disease. With the cooperative system we can properly apportion our resources. Here in the brigade, we are now twenty health-care workers at various levels. All of the six workteams, as well as the special units, receive health care. Seven or eight times a year we take general precautionary measures. We vaccinate against diphtheria, whooping cough, encephalitis, and type-B measles. We give pills against polio. In addition we check the privies and the pigsties and see to it that hygienic standards are kept up and improved.

"I am convinced that the cooperative medical system is the right solution. Proof is that in 1969 we had about ten or more people coming to the clinic everyday. Now there are only four or five. The reason for this is that, working within the collective system, we visit and examine each household twice a year. We give everyone a checkup. This means that we can take preventive measures in time. We can prevent many diseases, which, under a profit-oriented health-care system would develop into real and serious illnesses before the patient saw a doctor.

"Another of the tasks of collective medicine is to help the brigade members with family planning. We make propaganda for late marriage and few children. Men should not get married until they are twenty-five, and women not before twenty-three.

"There are 198 women of child-bearing age in the brigade. Of them 168 are fertile. Of this group 10 have been sterilized, 72 use an intrauterine device, 51 take birth-control pills, and 14 use condoms or the like. Eighty-nine percent of the couples take precautionary measures.

"We are now pushing for one child per family. If a woman becomes pregnant a second time, we recommend that she have an abortion within the first three months. This is performed at the commune's hospital. The women who have abortions are given fourteen days leave of absence from their jobs. During this period, they continue to receive their normal allotment of workpoints. Thus, the leave is paid for by the collective.

"We have now also begun an antismoking campaign. But air pollution has become much worse. In its wake it has brought several cases of bronchial infection. The children are especially vulnerable. The cement factory has begun taking countermeasures, in order to reduce pollution.

"The incidence of stomach and intestinal diseases has diminished. There are several reasons for this. One is better eating habits. We have recommended a more modern diet. In addition, the water has become cleaner, and the general standard of hygiene has improved. This is due to the campaigns we have carried out. Four times a year we hold campaigns for cleanliness, pure water, and the struggle against dirt and flies. We now also add iodine to the salt sold in the area. But the children still have a hard time observing the rules of hygiene and learning not to put things in their mouths, so they suffer from worms and parasites. We are trying to prevent this through education. We visit the school and talk about the importance of cleanliness and show pictures of the various parasites one can pick up if one isn't careful. Those who are infected are given vermicide.

"One good thing in recent years is that continuation courses for us health-care workers have been systematized. Every team has its own health-care workers. They have received a basic education in first aid and the like. They are now able to attend courses and continue their training. On passing an examination, they become barefoot doctors, capable of dealing with various simpler disorders, and are able to judge which cases they can handle by themselves. The examination is administered by the district and consists of a written and an oral section as well as a practical test under the supervision of an examiner.

"The barefoot doctors can then continue with their studies to become country doctors. This means that one reaches higher professional school level. I myself did these studies here at the hospital in this district. They consisted of an extended period of theoretical instruction and hospital practice. The major portion of the examination dealt with questions of diagnostics. I admitted patients, examined them, and then ordered treatment. I took part in four yearly one-month courses. These studies have helped me a lot. They have given me more self-confidence and insight. I also regularly study *The Shaanxi Medical Journal.* It appears four times a year and reports new developments, as well as interesting cases. It is also now part of my duty as a country doctor to supervise and assist the health-care workers in their continuing studies.

"This year, the municipality of Yanan has introduced a college-level medical education, lasting six months to a year, which is intended for experienced country doctors. We country doctors have devised a plan for how we all can have a turn at this course. After taking that examination, one is a general practitioner. There is then a higher level of study in the larger cities, for those who continue their education."

WITH ELEVEN GROTTOES, THE FAMILY IS NOW BETTER OFF

Fu Haicao says: "We're better off. The family now has eleven grottoes—four earth grottoes and seven tunnel-vaulted dwellings of stone. We have also built a house. I take care of the fifth workteam's horses and donkeys. I get ten workpoints a day. There are ten of us in the family, and all of us work. Life is getting better and better.

"I now have twelve grandchildren. My married son has six children and my married daughter also has six. Five of the grandchildren are boys and seven are girls. It's mostly for my grandchildren that I sing. Sometimes when I'm singing, other children come to listen. On occasion I've been asked to sing for the brigade. But, as I said, I mainly sing for my grandchildren.

"Some of my grandchildren go to school, while others are still too young and are at home. This year we built four stone grottoes. Last year we earned 6,000 jin of grain and 1,000 ￥ in cash. Besides this, we sold vegetables for 200 ￥ from our private plot, along with two of our own pigs for 300 ￥. We put aside 2,000 jin of grain to have in reserve, and we have money in the bank, too. We eat our own vegetables and our own pigs, the family sticks together, and everything is going really well."

Luo Hanhong has now been the leader of the second workteam since 1979. He sums up the experiences of the reorganization of agriculture in recent years: "We plow deeply and fertilize a mu with 2,000 jin of composted night soil, cow manure, and sheep droppings, together with 30 jin of phosphate and 30 to 45 jin of nitrate. We have found this to be the most effective combination. You can say that costs have increased, but then so have yields. It's worth it. We have now got all of Yanan to begin cultivating a better variety of wheat and to adopt more modern methods. About 800,000 mu are being cultivated according to new techniques. The fact is that if people see that a method gives good results, they'll accept it, even if it means a little extra work and a little more money. The system of responsibility allows us to decide more for ourselves. The brigade just assigns us a target.

"I have five children. The three eldest work in agriculture. The boy is nineteen, and the girls are seventeen and fifteen. The younger two, my eleven-year-old girl and eight-year-old boy, go to school. The two eldest are now ready to become members of the youth association. It makes no difference that the children work in my team. When they do a good job, I praise them, just like I would anyone else, and when they do a poor job, I criticize them.

"At home we study so that the children will better understand society. Since March of this year we in our family have been observing 'the five emphases':

"Emphasis on propriety (civilization, culture),
"Emphasis on hygiene,
"Emphasis on order (general discipline),
"Emphasis on politeness and courtesy, and
"Emphasis on morality.

"And we have also studied the 'four cleanlinesses':

"Cleanliness of spirit,
"Cleanliness of language,
"Cleanliness of behavior, and
"Cleanliness of environment.

"As we all know, young people are not born knowing how to behave. It is the duty of the family to provide them with a moral foundation on which to stand. That is what we are doing in this campaign for socialist ethics.

"We still live in the same old grottoes. But we have had the four grottoes reinforced with beams. However, we are now planning to build new dwellings. I have already had 30,000 bricks formed and fired. We are going to build tunnel-vaulted houses of brick.

We are going to build five such dwellings. We have the money for it. I have also put 4,000 jin of grain in reserve. I have given my wife and my eldest son wristwatches. I have bought a bicycle and a radio. Last year I bought two big cupboards and a proper chest of drawers. I am waiting to buy a sewing machine, until I can get a good brand. It's true that there are now lots of bicycles and sewing machines in the shops, and that people have a lot of money to spend, but the bicycles and sewing machines on the market are of poor and local manufacture. People look down on those who buy this stuff. It's like the difference between real cloth and homespun. No one wants to be seen in clothing made of homespun material. People look down on anyone who does go around like that. It's the same with bicycles and sewing machines. Price is of no great consequence. When it comes to bicycles, it's got to be a genuine Flying Dove from Shanghai, or at least an Eternity. Otherwise, forget it."

PEOPLE AND CHANGES

In the years prior to the Cultural Revolution, two youths from Liu Lin had gone to do advanced studies. Neither of them were from a Liu Lin workteam. During the Cultural Revolution, two worker-peasant-soldier-students were sent to college from Liu Lin Brigade. These were Liu Dequin and Cao Zhengui's daughter, Cao Aiping, who studied at Xian's Institute of Telecommunications.

In the years following 1976 seven young people had gone on to higher studies, and, of these, three had graduated. Of the seven youths, three were from Liu Lin itself, from families portrayed in previous reports:

> Feng Changye's daughter, Feng Guangling, had graduated from Yanan Medical Institute.
> Old Secretary Li Youhua's grandson, Li Zhigang, the son of Li Haifa, was now studying at Xian's Technical High School.
> The daughter of Liu Zhenrong and Li Yangqin (the housewife), Liu Lancun, had attended the teachers college in Yanan and now worked as a nursery school teacher.

Of the six persons from Liu Lin Brigade who are now party or government cadres outside of Liu Lin, four were already cadres back in 1962. They have, however, advanced in rank:

> Li Haijun was in charge of Liu Lin People's Commune's savings and loan association in 1962 and is now assistant manager of Yanan's Building Department.
> Li Haizhen was manager of Liu Lin's District Agricultural Tool Factory and is now director of Yanan's Institute for Forestry Research.
> Ren Tewan, who was party secretary for Yanan Pottery, is now party secretary of Yuanlong People's Commune.

People and Changes

Xue Tongli (Tian Guihua's husband), who was party secretary for Yanan's coal mines, is now department head at the state construction office in Yanan.

In these twenty years, three people from Liu Lin have advanced from political posts within the brigade to positions as political cadres:

Feng Changye is now deputy party secretary for Liu Lin People's Commune.
Cao Zhengui is now party secretary for Date Orchard People's Commune.
Liu Deqin is deputy mayor of Yanan.

(By the way, the enthusiastic young teacher, Wang Shijie, from 1969, is now a factory worker in Xian.)

This is a stable brigade in a stable people's commune, situated in one of the old liberated base areas, which has enjoyed settled political situation down through the years. Liu Deqin, with whom I had such heated arguments in 1969 (she was, in fact, still rather naive and inexperienced, as Cao Zhengui said at the time), now fetches me at the brigade to go eat dinner and take in a movie in the company of Yanan's leading cadres. She says, "I have often thought about our discussions in 1969. I understand better now. I have often talked with comrades about this afterward."

'At dinner, she again raised the issue. The mayor cut in to confirm what she had said: She had discussed these questions with them on several occasions.)

"In October 1970 I was recommended for study at Qinghua University in Peking. I studied there for three and a half years and graduated in 1974. We cadres were supposed to return to our villages and towns, and in 1975 I came back here. I became party secretary for a suburban people's commune and continued in that

143

position until 1978, when I was elected deputy chairman of Yanan's revolutionary committee. Now that the revolutionary committee has been transformed into an organ of municipal government, I am assistant mayor, in charge of educational, cultural, and health affairs.

"We suffer a shortage of nursery schools. In Yanan we have two day-care centers for slightly older children, and one for infants. We are now trying to encourage various institutions and workplaces to invest money in opening day nurseries. But it is not always so easy.

"In the archeological survey of all of Yanan County, which we are presently carrying out, we have been able to chart the Buddhist grottoes and monuments. These caves and grottoes are to be found in every commune. It is important to have them catalogued."

A large portrait of Mao Zedong covers the far wall of the reception room where I sit. It is an old portrait. I had seen pictures of Mao Zedong in the homes of some of the older peasants of Liu Lin. But this was the only large portrait of Mao I had seen displayed in a public building on this visit to China.

Party secretary Yang Chunrong said: "Yes, we have a stable corps of cadres here in Yanan, but it is now necessary to foster younger ones. Our most important task will be to train new cadres among the grass roots. Yanan is to remain an agricultural center, with but a limited amount of industry. We are now in the process of carrying out the necessary reorganization. Aside from agriculture, stock raising and forestry will be our most important industries. To promote these sectors of the economy, we intend to offer training in agricultural engineering here. We shall establish a number of schools.

"The railroad is going to be built. It has just been temporarily delayed due to the general economic readjustment. This only means that it has been slightly postponed. We are continuing with our planning. The new station is to be built below Liu Lin. The plans are all ready.

"It is still rather uncertain what the future holds in store for Liu Lin. As you know, the brigade lies to the west and is not well suited for vegetable cultivation. It will probably become a service brigade for the city. One presumes that it will continue growing fruit, and even share in the responsibility of supplying the city with meat."

CONVERSATION IN THE CAPITAL

On the way to Peking the countryside is a panorama beyond the window of the train. Distant villages remain visible a long while—perhaps a minute. Closer villages enter the scene from the left and disappear to the right. The wheels pound against the rail joints, and the railway car lurches in the curves. Continually, there are villages, fields, more villages, occasional clumps of trees, and here and there a canal that cuts across my field of vision, only to disappear once more. And groups of men who lift their eyes and look at the train. I catch a glimpse of their faces, and then they are gone.

Conditions in some of these villages are perhaps as they once were in Fengyang District. Or as I was told they once were. I never understood, and still do not understand, why things should have been so wretched there. I can think of various possible explanations, but I know too little to understand. Still, I heard enough to make me wonder about the future. It is surely a delusion to think that people who are poor and struggling to survive, like the majority of Fengyang's inhabitants, would be filled with enthusiasm and confidence in the future just because a few individuals got rich and to believe that they would catch the spirit from these successes, and so themselves become rich. It is especially unlikely, since the newly rich model peasants are party members, the same people who but recently were foremen, bookkeepers, and leaders of the collective.

But perhaps the problem was that the peasants of Fengyang District were lazy? Yet, I have a rather difficult time believing in the laziness of the peasantry. The idea that people idle about reveals, as Mao would say, a very definite class standpoint. Perhaps in the past they had not found it worthwhile to work. Or maybe they now have no other choice but to get up and go to the fields several hours earlier each morning, and go home to eat and sleep a few hours later than in the past. There are, to be sure, old, well-tried methods to make people sweat, but such methods generally end badly for some of those on high.

Provided that there is not something unexplained or hidden, and that the system now being introduced in Fengyang is to hold sway over China's 800 million rural inhabitants, I actually believe that the bitter old veteran will be proven correct. But how, when, or under what banner, it is impossible to predict.

I know enough about one brigade in China to be able to see the pattern clearly. There are other brigades similar to Liu Lin. I know this for a fact. For example, Fenghuo Brigade, which I also visited on this trip. It, too, is located in Shaanxi, but close to Xian. Unlike Liu Lin, it has, during various periods, served as a national model. I had also visited it in the past. There, too, hung portraits of Mao Zedong in the rooms of the cadres. Mao himself had also shown an interest in Fenghuo, way back in the 1950s. They, too, had adjusted to the new agricultural policies, but without going to extremes. And the main thoroughfare of the village (which was almost a small town) was still named Antirevisionist Street. The street had been given that name in 1975, when the brigade had been learning from Dazhai, and when, through its own efforts, it had built up a collective serving the people. Compared with Liu Lin, this was a rich brigade in a rich agricultural district. The peasants of Fenghuo were beginning to acquire television sets. They, too, had begun using production quotas and special contracts, but the collective remained in existence. I cannot say much, however, about their internal contradictions. Nonetheless, if a large number of the villages that flew by my train window in what looked like an endless procession were like Liu Lin or Fenghuo, or if they, at least, significantly resemble Liu Lin and Fenghuo, then I do not believe that the bitter old veteran was right. There will be no need, in that case, to start again from the beginning. The caliber of the people leading the collectives may vary, and their solutions may turn out different, but after this period of increased distribution, there will inevitably follow a new period of mass campaigns and accumulation. Perhaps not in the same form as those of 1959–1960 or 1968–1970, but spurred by the same driving forces. There will then be enough people who will demand a collective effort at organizing the irrigation systems better (as in 1959–1960) or who will demand collective investments in mechanization and construction (as in 1968–1970). The ideological vestments will undoubtedly be different, but the profound and rational thought behind the Great Leap Forward or the Cultural Revolution will light the way.

Yet, it is also possible that what we are now witnessing is the beginnings of a new class differentiation in the countryside, and that the leadership actually has been as bad as Fengyang's must have been, and that we are going to see a new division into a half-starving, redundant mass of poor peasants, on the one hand, and a few million successful (and rich) peasants of a new type, on the other. Perhaps, like the craftsmen in the cities, these new rich peasants will even be allowed (or will force through) the right to employ two assistant workers and five apprentices. These will, of course, come from among the poor peasant masses.

Beyond the train window the villages speed past. Here and there, men lift their gaze from the field to look at the train. I glimpse their faces for one brief moment. Then they are gone again.

The perspective as viewed from the center of power is another. I know that. But it is not from on high that one is able to get a comprehensive view. There the opinions shift according to the various power constellations. I have read what the leaders say and write. I have also talked with those in power and heard the nuances, heard that which is not always published or has not yet been published or is no longer published. Perhaps there are leaders whose opinions differ from the official line, but if so, we will find out about it tomorrow, or next year, or in ten years, or else (providing the documents are not falsified) the historians will learn of it in one hundred years.

But it is not the leaders who are going to decide the future. Their policies and decisions do not govern developments. They are symptoms; they enhance tendencies. The only leading political leader in the true sense was Mao Zedong, and he was a leader not because of his political and military decisions (although even they were important, and played a crucial role on that level where political and military decisions are important), but because of his ability to gather and express simple and (what later seemed to be) self-evident thoughts and needs. This great method was his—a method impossible to capture in a dogma.

Here I deliberately disassociate myself with what is now being said in China about Mao Zedong's works and Mao Zedong Thought. I am of the opinion that Mao Zedong's life work does actually represent a Maoism—not just the application of Marxism-Leninism on actual Chinese conditions. It goes without saying that his political thinking was related to actual Chinese condition. Otherwise, it would have been worthless. But he was an innovator, just as was Marx in his time. The fact that Mao, seeing those who wanted to be Maoists, declared that he himself was certainly no Maoist, is no stranger than that Marx, upon considering the Marxists of his own day, felt that whatever he was, he was no Marxist. Both Marx and Mao represent new stages. Before Marx the issues were posed one way, after him another; before Mao, one way, after him another.

However, I do not discuss this when I am in Peking. They know my opinion. I know the officially established truth about Mao Zedong. I believe it false. My hosts know this, I know they know it, and there is nothing more to say. I can obviously not decree any truths in Peking, or anywhere else for that matter, and the situation in Peking again resembles that prior to the Cultural Revolution, when truths were decreed and considered gospel at the fall of the chairman's gavel.

I speak with an old friend. We have known each other for thirty years. My friend is not a party member, and never has been. He is a patriotic, progressive Chinese intellectual, a sympathizer, who has been close to the party for almost forty years.

"At liberation, we danced in the streets. Oh, how we danced and were happy."

But that was a long time ago now, and my friend wonders if I cannot help some of his relatives get residence and work permits in Sweden. They are already well educated technicians at an advanced level.

"Sweden should have some use for them."

"Are they unemployed?" I ask.

"No, they aren't unemployed, not with their educations, but they would like very much to work in Sweden or the United States."

Return to a Chinese Village

My friend hates the Cultural Revolution. Not because it harmed his family physically, with stabs and blows and thefts; it didn't. In fact, Zhou Enlai personally protected the family, since it was useful to China, and my friend never needed to attend cadre school or even move from his house in Peking. But the Cultural Revolution had meant that some of his relatives had had to work in the countryside for several years.

"Their education suffered. One of them did not get into the university after that. Evening courses were not for him. He has become a driver."

It is the first time in many generations that anyone in the family had become anything beside an intellectual and functionary. The Cultural Revolution demeaned them as an intellectual family and transformed one of its younger members into a worker. This my friend will never forgive. And it is Mao Zedong who is never to be forgiven.

"He was responsible."

I tell him about Liu Lin, and about the work there, the cadres and the stability.

"Just you wait. They'll be purged. Those who took part in the Cultural Revolution are going to be swept away with an iron broom. The party is now going to commence a real purge. They're finally going to get theirs!"

I try to tell him something about how Liu Deqin has matured, but my friend just says contentedly, "Yes, such people are going to be purged. She's going to have to go back to work in the fields!"

Still, this is a close, old friend, and we should be able to talk to each other. But no words or arguments touch him. My friend is an intellectual, and full of hate.

I meet authors. We drink wine. We eat and converse. I have read some of their writing, and they are not bad. But they do not write about the people I have met and become acquainted with through the years. They talk to me mostly about the Pen Club, and about various Pen writers, and about the Pen meetings around the world they have attended, or are going to attend.

I wonder how they depict Chinese reality, and I tell them a story about a girl who dreams of going to school but who instead must stay home and care for her sickly father; about how she marries a man who moves in with the father; how she takes care of her husband, who is nice to be sure but hardly interested in what his wife dreamed of as a girl; and about how she has children and pulls the heavy millstone and thinks about how her children's future will be; and how the children then do not care at all about school, how they become lazy pupils and not even good peasants. All this I know because I have known her for twenty years and heard the story. I ask them if they describe fates such as this, and how they go about it. But they just laugh self-consciously and say:

"Yes, there is that kind of backward area, where such things do occur. But if you had visited the brigades around Peking and Shanghai, you would have been spared this experience. Around here, everyone can go to school and train themselves to become what they like."

I tell them other stories. I tell them about the little counter-revolutionary, about how he hid himself but was taken to the camp and then came back, and about how he almost got into trouble again by being obliging on the occasion of a new campaign, and about his son's bitterness, and how he had been given back his civil rights, but that the old antagonisms still remained. And they say, "All the old labels have been taken away, but naturally there are those who still cling to ultraleftist attitudes, when it comes to dealing with people once labeled this or that."

After a few more attempts, I give up. They are not interested. They are not even interested when I tell them what people in Liu Lin thought about the new films, the ones about love and about how pretty young people water ski and the like. (I had, in fact, gone to the movies in Yanan and seen such films in the company of cadres and villagers from Liu Lin. Their faces had been as if chiseled from stone. They did not smile at any of the witticisms about the love between the ne'er-do-well at the factory and the manager's spoiled daughter.) All my colleagues have to say is:

"Yes, there are backward areas where the people have not yet learned to appreciate what's modern."

The day before our departure from Peking, Gun and I are standing on the balcony to our room at the Peking Hotel. It is morning, and down below, the street is filled with buses, swarms of bicyclists, and an occasional car. These are thousands and thousands of functionaries, on their way to their offices in the ancient capital of the world's most populous nation—a country possessing the world's eldest intellectual bureaucratic tradition.

"The capital is growing," says Gun. "Down there, the government officials are heading for their departments, while around the city, unemployed youth are waiting to find a way in through the back door of some department or institution, since it is both more pleasant and more honorable to be unemployed in Peking, than to dig the earth out in the boondocks."

"These unemployed youth have attended school and are some kind of intellectuals," I said. "They are utterly convinced that Mao Zedong was not just mistaken when he urged them to go out into the countryside, learn to stand on their own two feet, and contribute to the building of China, but also that these beliefs of his were reactionary as well as harmful, and that no worse fate could befall go-ahead youth than that of having to spend time among the peasantry."

"Yes," said Gun, "so we're now back to India. And Mao's fate is to be the same as Gandhi's. Gandhi argued that it was necessary to break the castes, and his volunteers were obliged to clean the privies. Mao used the same method, for the same reasons. And now they are both dead, and transformed into national saints—but the castes remain."

"The question is, however, are we in an India lacking Naxalites?" I say.

"How are we to know that?" asks Gun. "We wouldn't be able to meet them, if there were any."

"But that's nothing to be disappointed about," I say. "This, too, Mao foresaw. China's people stood up and in doing so shook the world. Later, the situation changed and new contradictions arose. There'll be new uprisings in the future. And even if the very name Mao Zedong were to be forgotten, people would still know even a thousand and ten thousand years from now that it is right to make revolution."

GLOSSARY

Explanation of Terms Used in the Text

fen	A coin, the 100th part of a yuan.
jin	A unit of weight. A jin is equal to 1 pound, 1½ ounces, or 500 grams.
KMT	Guomindang (Kuomintang), a middle-class democratic national party, formed in 1912 by Sun Yat-sen. Later joined the Comintern, when China's Communist Party became a part of the Guomindang. Sun Yat-sen died in March 1925. Finally, when the Guomindang seemed to be victorious all over the country, Chiang Kai-shek carried out his long-planned attack on the communists and leftist elements in the so-called big "April Massacres" of 1927. The ultimate result of this action was Chiang Kai-shek's flight to Taiwan in 1949 together with the remnants of the Guomindang.
loess	Layers of fertile wind-blown yellow soil. Its grain size is 0.0008–0.0015 inch. Loess forms huge deposits in which the rain cuts deep ravines.
mu	A unit of area. A mu is equal to 0.1518 acre, or $\frac{1}{15}$ hectare.
yuan (¥)	The basic monetary unit in China. As of December 12, 1982), 1 ¥ was equal to $0.52 in U.S. dollars.

About the Author

Jan Myrdal has written seven books on China and Asia, five of them in collaboration with his wife, Gun Kessle. His autobiography, *Confessions of a Disloyal European,* received considerable attention. In addition, he has published novels, books of essays, and a collection of radio plays in Sweden, where his weekly column is a continual source of controversy. He is currently editing the novels of Balzac in Sweden and has made several television documentaries.

Myrdal's most recent book, *The Silk Road: A Journey from the High Pamirs and Ili through Sinkiang and Kansu,* with photographs by Gun Kessle, was published by Pantheon in 1980.